Computer Users' Data

PROFESSIONAL AND INDUSTRIAL COMPUTING SERIES

Consulting Editors

DAN SIMPSON
BSc, FIMA, FBCS
Alvey Directorate

RICHARD VERYARD
MA, MSc
Data Logic Limited

The aim of this series is to address various practical issues and topics in information technology. Modern computing involves a growing number of specialist areas; it is increasingly difficult to keep one's knowledge current. The emphasis is on providing up-to-date coverage of a subject, rather than theoretical novelty. These books should be widely read by practising professionals in data processing and information technology, as well as by students on vocational courses, in order to maintain and improve professional standards of computing in industry and commerce. The authors themselves are drawn either directly from industry or are academics with first-hand industrial/commercial experience.

Computer Users' Data Book

B.C. WALSH
BSc, PhD, MBLS
Department of
Computer Science
University of Liverpool

J.L. SCHONFELDER
MSc, DIC, PhD, MBCS, AFIMA
Computer Laboratory
University of Liverpool

P.H. JESTY
MSc, MBCS
Department of
Computer Studies
University of Leeds

M.D. BEER
BSc, PhD
Department of
Computer Science
University of Liverpool

BLACKWELL SCIENTIFIC PUBLICATIONS

OXFORD   LONDON   EDINBURGH

BOSTON   PALO ALTO   MELBOURNE

© 1986 by
Blackwell Scientific Publications
Editorial Offices:
Osney Mead, Oxford, OX2 0EL
8 John Street, London, WC1N 2ES
23 Ainslie Place, Edinburgh, EH3 6AJ
52 Beacon Street, Boston
   Massachusetts 02108, USA
667 Lytton Avenue, Palo Alto
   California 94301, USA
107 Barry Street, Carlton
   Victoria 3053, Australia

First published 1986

Phototypeset by
Oxford Computer Typesetting

Printed and bound in
Great Britain by
Hollen Street Press
Slough, Berkshire

Distributed in North America by
Blackwell Scientific Publications Inc.
PO Box 50009, Palo Alto
California 94303, USA

British Library
Cataloguing in Publication Data

Computer users' data book.
  1. Electronic data processing
  I. Walsh, B.C.
004   QA76

  ISBN 0-632-01179-3 pbk
  ISBN 0-632-01608-6 hbk

Contents

Foreword

The aim of this book is to provide immediately accessible information on a wide range of data relating to computers and their usage. It is an indispensable ready reference which belongs on the desk of every computer professional, in the pocket of every student and next to every computer terminal.

The authors have extracted the important and relevant features from the vast body of computer lore and presented the results in a concise yet readable form. Limitations of space meant that difficult choices had to be made on this book's contents. However, if you would like to see other material included in future editions, or have noticed any errors, would you please send your comments to:

Dr M.D. Beer
Department of Computer Science
Chadwick Tower
University of Liverpool
P.O. Box 147
Liverpool L69 3BX

Chapter One
Information Representation

The basic representation of information in virtually all modern digital computers is in terms of 'bits'. The computer works by having a number of electronic elements which can be set into one of two states, called 'on' or 'off', '0' or '1', 'false' or 'true', etc., according to the interpretation that is appropriate. The term 'bit' is used to describe one such binary state device. One bit is the smallest possible unit of information that can be stored. All items of information that are stored and processed by computers are coded into one or more bits.

Two bits taken together can have four different states, represented by the different combinations of the two-bit values, viz. 00, 01, 10, 11. These could be used to code for the values 1, 2, 3, 4; directions north, south, east, west; letters A, B, C, D, etc. — in fact anything that has four exclusive categories. Three bits similarly code for eight different states, four bits for 16, and so on.

The number of values, states or objects that can be coded into a given number of bits is two raised to the power of the number of bits. That is, if n is the number of bits, then N, the number of different values that can be coded by this number of bits, is given by

$$N = 2^n$$

Conversely, if we have a set of N different objects to be coded we will need at least

$$n = [\log_2 N]$$

bits to code them for storage on a computer (the notation $[a]$ means the smallest integer greater than or equal to a).

Most computers do not store information in memory, or retrieve it, as single bits since single binary choices are not that common in data. It is much more common to want groups, or a string, of bits which code for characters (letters, numerals, etc.) or numeric values. Therefore, the computer works with various sizes of groups of bits which it can address in memory and can store and retrieve as a single operation. The smallest unit that can normally be addressed on most computers is termed the

1

'byte' which is 8 bits. This is usually used to code characters. The larger groups of bits that can be directly addressed are then called words and usually code numeric values. The size of a word varies from computer to computer and on one computer there may be more than one word size depending on the nature of the data being stored.

Some mainframe computers cannot directly address small groups of bits independently and always work with relatively large 'whole words' of storage at a time. Such computers usually allow sub-strings of bits within a word to be interpreted as characters.

1.1 Word Sizes of Common Computer Types and Microprocessors

Byte Computers

These computers all use an 8-bit byte as the smallest addressable unit of storage, and a byte is used to store a single character coded into binary. All such computers support word sizes which are an integral number of bytes.

Short or half word	= 2 bytes, 16 bits
Word	= 4 bytes, 32 bits
Long or double word	= 8 bytes, 64 bits

On the larger mainframe computers with this sort of structure it is common also to have a quadword = 16 bytes, 128 bits.

Virtually all microprocessors are byte computers (see Section 2.3). The common 8-bit processors, such as the 6502, Z80, 8080 and 6800 families of microprocessors, retrieve information for store a byte at a time.

The 16-bit processors, such as the Z8000, 8086, 68000, and LSI/11 families of microprocessors, are so called because they retrieve information 16-bits at a time. The DEC PDP 11 and Hewlett-Packard 3000 are minicomputers with this property. Most byte-based minicomputers or mainframes can retrieve information 32-bits or a word at a time. Machines in this category include:

IBM 370, 4300, 3030, 3080
ICL 2900 (VME computers)
DEC VAX
Prime
GEC 4000
Data General MV series
Honeywell DPS7

Word Computers

Other word sizes in common use for mainframe word-based computers but not for microprocessors are:

24-bit word
    ICL 1900, ME29, 2900 (DME computers)
    HARRIS
36-bit word
    DEC 10, 20
    Honeywell Level 66 and Multics
    Univac 1100
60-bit word
    CDC Cyber 170, 7600
    CRAY
64-bit word
    CDC Cyber 205

1.2 Binary Representation of Integers

1.2.1 Positive Values

Since n-bits can code for 2^n different data values, n-bits can be used to represent the positive integers from zero to $2^n - 1$. This coding is usually done by interpreting the bits as digits in a conventional positional number system with radix or base 2. That is, if we had 3 bits we would interpret the possible bit patterns as:

$$000 = 0 \times 4 + 0 \times 2 + 0 \times 1 = 0$$
$$001 = 0 \times 4 + 0 \times 2 + 1 \times 1 = 1$$
$$010 = 0 \times 4 + 1 \times 2 + 0 \times 1 = 2$$
$$011 = 0 \times 4 + 1 \times 2 + 1 \times 1 = 3$$
$$100 = 1 \times 4 + 0 \times 2 + 0 \times 1 = 4 \ldots$$

$$\ldots 111 = 1 \times 4 + 1 \times 2 + 1 \times 1 = 7$$

Similarly, for 4 bits we represent the values from 0 to $2^4 - 1 = 15$ as:

$$0000 = 0 \times 8 + 0 \times 4 + 0 \times 2 + 0 \times 1 = 0 \ldots$$

$$\ldots 0111 = 0 \times 8 + 1 \times 4 + 1 \times 2 + 1 \times 1 = 7$$
$$1000 = 1 \times 8 + 0 \times 4 + 0 \times 2 + 0 \times 1 = 8 \ldots$$

$$\ldots 1111 = 1 \times 8 + 1 \times 4 + 1 \times 2 + 1 \times 1 = 15$$

If we count the bits from the right as $b_0, b_1, \ldots b_{n-1}$ then the general relationship for the value a, represented by a bit string of length n, is

$$a = \sum_{i=0}^{n-1} b_i \, 2^i$$

N.B. In a binary number the digits b_i can take only the values 0 or 1.

Binary numbers, being rather long strings of 0- or 1-bit values, are very tedious to write down and also very easy to get wrong. Therefore, when working in binary it is normal to actually write values in a larger number base such as 8, octal, or 16, hexadecimal (hex). In the former, each octal digit converts directly to a group of 3 bits in the binary value, and in the latter, each hex digit converts to a group of 4 bits.

Table 1.1. Octal — binary conversion.

Binary	Octal digits
000	0
001	1
010	2
011	3
100	4
101	5
110	6
111	7

Binary numbers are so seldom written out in full that no conventional notation is used for them. The fact that strings of 1s and 0s are binary numbers and not decimal is normally clear from the context. Octal numbers can often not be distinguished easily from the context. They are, therefore, often distinguished by a trailing subscript 8 or the number is preceded or followed by some special symbol which indicates that the digits are to be interpreted as octal. There is little agreement among manufacturers as to what symbol should be used, or whether it should precede or follow. In this book we shall use the symbol £ in front of a string of digits to indicate that this is an octal number and not decimal.

Using Table 1.1 the following conversions may be made

$$£173 \qquad = \text{binary } 1111011$$
$$= 123 \text{ decimal}$$

$$\text{binary } 110101001 = £651$$

Table 1.2. Hexadecimal — binary.

Binary	Hex
0000	0
0001	1
0010	2
0011	3
0100	4
0101	5
0110	6
0111	7
1000	8
1001	9
1010	A
1011	B
1100	C
1101	D
1110	E
1111	F

Hex numbers will be denoted in this book by the symbol & preceding the digits. Also, since the radix of the number system is 16, there must be 16 digit symbols. Conventionally the usual digits 0–9 are used with their normal digit values and the letters A–F are used to represent digit values of 10–15.

Using Table 1.2 the following conversions may be made

&75 = binary 01110101 = decimal 117 = £165
binary 1001111101010011 = &9F53

Because of the very common use of the 8-bit byte as a fundamental unit for many aspects of modern computing, hexadecimal is used now more frequently than octal; two hexdigits represent a byte. Octal is now used mainly on systems which use 6-bit characters, and these are becoming increasingly rare. Hence in what follows we shall concentrate on hex.

1.2.2 Conversion of Hexadecimal Numbers

The tables in this section provide direct conversion for numbers between hexadecimal and decimal.

Table 1.3. Hex-decimal conversion.

Value	Digits-position							
	1st	2nd	3rd	4th	5th	6th	7th	8th
1	1	16	256	4096	65536	1048576	16777216	268435456
2	2	32	512	8192	131072	2097152	33554432	536870912
3	3	48	768	12288	196608	3145728	50331648	805306368
4	4	64	1024	16384	262144	4194304	67108864	1073741824
5	5	80	1280	20480	327680	5242880	83886080	1342177280
6	6	96	1536	24576	393216	6291456	100663296	1610612736
7	7	112	1792	28672	458752	7340032	117440512	1879048192
8	8	128	2048	32768	524288	8388608	134217728	2147483648
9	9	144	2304	36864	589824	9437184	150994944	2415919104
A	10	160	2560	40960	655360	10485760	167772160	2684354560
B	11	176	2816	45056	720896	11534336	184549376	2952790016
C	12	192	3072	49152	786432	12582912	201326592	3221225472
D	13	208	3328	53248	851968	13631488	218103808	3489660928
E	14	224	3584	57344	917504	14680064	234881024	3758096384
F	15	240	3840	61440	983040	15728640	251658240	4026531840

Using Table 1.3 the hex value &DA29C =

```
     12
    144
    512
  40960
 851968
 893596
```

(decimal addition)

Table 1.4. Decimal – hex conversion.

Value	10th	9th	8th	7th	6th	5th	4th	3rd	2nd	1st
				Digits-position						
1	3B9ACA00	5F5E100	989680	F4240	186A0	2710	3E8	64	A	1
2	7359400	BEBC200	1312D00	1E8480	30D40	4E20	7D0	C8	14	2
3	B2D05E00	11E1A300	1C9C380	2DC6C0	493E0	7530	BB8	12C	1E	3
4	EE6B2800	17D78400	2625A00	3D0900	61A80	9C40	FA0	190	28	4
5	12A05F200	1DCD6500	2FAF080	4C4B40	7A120	C350	1388	1F4	32	5
6	165A0BC00	23C34600	3938700	5B8D80	927C0	EA60	1770	258	3C	6
7	1A13B8600	29B92700	42C1D80	6ACFC0	AAE60	11170	1B58	2BC	46	7
8	1DCD65000	2FAF0800	4C4B400	7A1200	C3500	13880	1F40	320	50	8
9	218711A00	35A4E900	55D4A80	895440	DBBA0	15F90	2328	384	5A	9

Using Table 1.4 the decimal value 4956 =

```
    &6
   &32        (hex addition)
  &384
  &FA0
  ------
 &135C
```

N.B. The addition here is done in hex, that is with a base of 16 not 10. This means that say

```
  &6                    &9
  &5          and       &8
  ------                ------
  &B  (not 11)          &11  (not 17)
```

The complete addition table for hex digits is given in Table 1.5.

Table 1.5. Hexadecimal arithmetic — addition table. Addition of two single digit hexadecimal values.

							Hexadecimal digit								
0	1	2	3	4	5	6	7	8	9	A	B	C	D	E	F
1	02	03	04	05	06	07	08	09	0A	0B	0C	0D	0E	0F	10
2	03	04	05	06	07	08	09	0A	0B	0C	0D	0E	0F	10	11
3	04	05	06	07	08	09	0A	0B	0C	0D	0E	0F	10	11	12
4	05	06	07	08	09	0A	0B	0C	0D	0E	0F	10	11	12	13
5	06	07	08	09	0A	0B	0C	0D	0E	0F	10	11	12	13	14
6	07	08	09	0A	0B	0C	0D	0E	0F	10	11	12	13	14	15
7	08	09	0A	0B	0C	0D	0E	0F	10	11	12	13	14	15	16
8	09	0A	0B	0C	0D	0E	0F	10	11	12	13	14	15	16	17
9	0A	0B	0C	0D	0E	0F	10	11	12	13	14	15	16	17	18
A	0B	0C	0D	0E	0F	10	11	12	13	14	15	16	17	18	19
B	0C	0D	0E	0F	10	11	12	13	14	15	16	17	18	19	1A
C	0D	0E	0F	10	11	12	13	14	15	16	17	18	19	1A	1B
D	0E	0F	10	11	12	13	14	15	16	17	18	19	1A	1B	1C
E	0F	10	11	12	13	14	15	16	17	18	19	1A	1B	1C	1D
F	10	11	12	13	14	15	16	17	18	19	1A	1B	1C	1D	1E

Hexadecimal digit

Table 1.6 (i). Hexadecimal–decimal (0–255) in the hex range (0–FF).

Hex 2nd digit	Hex 1st digit															
	0	1	2	3	4	5	6	7	8	9	A	B	C	D	E	F
00	0000	0001	0002	0003	0004	0005	0006	0007	0008	0009	0010	0011	0012	0013	0014	0015
10	0016	0017	0018	0019	0020	0021	0022	0023	0024	0025	0026	0027	0028	0029	0030	0031
20	0032	0033	0034	0035	0036	0037	0038	0039	0040	0041	0042	0043	0044	0045	0046	0047
30	0048	0049	0050	0051	0052	0053	0054	0055	0056	0057	0058	0059	0060	0061	0062	0063
40	0064	0065	0066	0067	0068	0069	0070	0071	0072	0073	0074	0075	0076	0077	0078	0079
50	0080	0081	0082	0083	0084	0085	0086	0087	0088	0089	0090	0091	0092	0093	0094	0095
60	0096	0097	0098	0099	0100	0101	0102	0103	0104	0105	0106	0107	0108	0109	0110	0111
70	0112	0113	0114	0115	0116	0117	0118	0119	0120	0121	0122	0123	0124	0125	0126	0127
80	0128	0129	0130	0131	0132	0133	0134	0135	0136	0137	0138	0139	0140	0141	0142	0143
90	0144	0145	0146	0147	0148	0149	0150	0151	0152	0153	0154	0155	0156	0157	0158	0159
A0	0160	0161	0162	0163	0164	0165	0166	0167	0168	0169	0170	0171	0172	0173	0174	0175
B0	0176	0177	0178	0179	0180	0181	0182	0183	0184	0185	0186	0187	0188	0189	0190	0191
C0	0192	0193	0194	0195	0196	0197	0198	0199	0200	0201	0202	0203	0204	0205	0206	0207
D0	0208	0209	0210	0211	0212	0213	0214	0215	0216	0217	0218	0219	0220	0221	0222	0223
E0	0224	0225	0226	0227	0228	0229	0230	0231	0232	0233	0234	0235	0236	0237	0238	0239
F0	0240	0241	0242	0243	0244	0245	0246	0247	0248	0249	0250	0251	0252	0253	0254	0255

The value of 7A is obtained by looking along the row 70 until the A column is reached. The decimal value is read as 122 (&7A = 122).

Table 1.6 (ii). Octal–decimal (0–255) in the octal range 0–377.

				Octal 1st digit				
	0	1	2	3	4	5	6	7
000	0000	0001	0002	0003	0004	0005	0006	0007
010	0008	0009	0010	0011	0012	0013	0014	0015
020	0016	0017	0018	0019	0020	0021	0022	0023
030	0024	0025	0026	0027	0028	0029	0030	0031
040	0032	0033	0034	0035	0036	0037	0038	0039
050	0040	0041	0042	0043	0044	0045	0046	0047
060	0048	0049	0050	0051	0052	0053	0054	0055
070	0056	0057	0058	0059	0060	0061	0062	0063
100	0064	0065	0066	0067	0068	0069	0070	0071
110	0072	0073	0074	0075	0076	0077	0078	0079
120	0080	0081	0082	0083	0084	0085	0086	0087
130	0088	0089	0090	0091	0092	0093	0094	0095
140	0096	0097	0098	0099	0100	0101	0102	0103
150	0104	0105	0106	0107	0108	0109	0110	0111
160	0112	0113	0114	0115	0116	0117	0118	0119
170	0120	0121	0122	0123	0124	0125	0126	0127
200	0128	0129	0130	0131	0132	0133	0134	0135
210	0136	0137	0138	0139	0140	0141	0142	0143
220	0144	0145	0146	0147	0148	0149	0150	0151
230	0152	0153	0154	0155	0156	0157	0158	0159
240	0160	0161	0162	0163	0164	0165	0166	0167
250	0168	0169	0170	0171	0172	0173	0174	0175
260	0176	0177	0178	0179	0180	0181	0182	0183
270	0184	0185	0186	0187	0188	0189	0190	0191
300	0192	0193	0194	0195	0196	0197	0198	0199
310	0200	0201	0202	0203	0204	0205	0206	0207
320	0208	0209	0210	0211	0212	0213	0214	0215
330	0216	0217	0218	0219	0220	0221	0222	0223
340	0224	0225	0226	0227	0228	0229	0230	0231
350	0232	0233	0234	0235	0236	0237	0238	0239
360	0240	0241	0242	0243	0244	0245	0246	0247
370	0248	0249	0250	0251	0252	0253	0254	0255

Octal 2nd and 3rd digits

Using Table 1.6 (ii) the value of £246 may be obtained by looking along the row 240 until the 6 column is reached. The decimal value is read as 166.

Table 1.7. Powers of 2 in decimal.

2^n	n	2^{-n}					
2	1	.5					
4	2	.25					
8	3	.125					
16	4	.062	5				
32	5	.031	25				
64	6	.015	625				
128	7	.007	812	5			
256	8	.003	906	25			
512	9	.001	953	125			
1 024	10	.000	976	562	5		
2 048	11	.000	488	281	25		
4 096	12	.000	244	140	625		
8 192	13	.000	122	070	312	5	
16 384	14	.000	061	035	156	25	
32 768	15	.000	030	517	578	125	
65 536	16	.000	015	258	789	062	5
131 072	17	.000	007	629	394	531	25
262 144	18	.000	003	814	697	265	625
524 288	19	.000	001	907	348	632	812
1 048 576	20	.000	000	953	674	316	406
2 097 152	21	.000	000	476	837	158	203
4 194 304	22	.000	000	238	418	579	101
8 388 608	23	.000	000	119	209	289	550
16 777 216	24	.000	000	059	604	644	775
33 554 432	25	.000	000	029	802	322	387
67 108 864	26	.000	000	014	901	161	193
134 217 728	27	.000	000	007	450	580	596
268 435 456	28	.000	000	003	725	290	298
536 870 912	29	.000	000	001	862	645	149
1 073 741 824	30	.000	000	000	931	322	574
2 147 483 648	31	.000	000	000	465	661	287

Using Table 1.7 the value of 2^8 is given to the left of the 8 in the centre column. It is 256. Similarly, 2^{-8} is read off on the right as .003 906 25. Values of 2^{-n} for n greater than 17 have been truncated after 18 decimal places.

Although the above tables are useful for helping hand calculation to perform the base conversions between decimal and hex representations, it will, in many cases, be easier to use an algorithm which can be programmed and a computer used to perform this task. Some computers make this extremely easy in that they provide both decimal and hex notations for the representation of integer values, plus a way of requesting that the value be printed out in one of these notations. For instance, the BBC micro BASIC language allows integer values either to be

represented as a normal decimal or as a hex value indicated by an &
preceding the digits. The display can then be requested in either form.
The program

  10   DEC% = dddd...

  20   PRINT   ~DEC%

where the list variable is produced by a tilde would cause the decimal
value represented by the decimal digit string dddd... to be printed in its
equivalent hex representation. The program

  10   HEX% = &hhhh...

  20   PRINT   HEX%

would cause the hex value represented by &hhhh... to be printed in its
equivalent decimal representation.

It should be noted that this will produce strange results if hex values
greater than 10^9, &3B9ACA00, are used because of precise details of
how the machine represents large values and negative numbers (see
next section).

Basically the algorithm for conversion of hex to decimal is simply to
evaluate the representational polynomial

$$a = \sum_{i=0} h_i(16)^i$$

where h_i are the hex digits 0–F with digits A–F given their decimal
values 10–15.

For decimal to hex conversion the technique is to divide repeatedly
by 16. At each division the remainder will give the hex digit value, the
zeroth digit from the first division, the first digit from the second and so
on.

Programming of both methods will cause difficulties if the numbers
being converted are large enough to nearly fill the word size used by the
computer to perform integer arithmetic.

The tables given here are sufficient to convert positive decimal
values to and from hex values that could be stored in 32 bits.

1.2.3 Positive and Negative Values

In any work with numeric values, which are not simply used to count or
code for objects, we must be able to perform arithmetic; in particular, to
be able to add and subtract values. We must, therefore, be able to

represent negative as well as positive values. To do this we must use one bit in the word to code for the sign of the value. In virtually all computer systems this is the leftmost bit of the word. If this bit is zero, the value is interpreted as positive. If this bit is one, the value is negative.

Virtually all systems, therefore, use n bits to represent integer values with $2^{n-1}-1$ as the largest positive representable value. That is, the leading bit, bit $n-1$, of zero represents a positive value. The remaining bits, bit 0 to bit $n-2$, represent the value as in the previous section. It would be possible to simply say that negative values were represented in the same way but with the leading bit of 1 indicating the value as negative. That is, a simple sign-modulus representation could be used. The value would be interpreted as

$$a = (-1)^{b_{n-1}} \sum_{i=0}^{n-2} b_i \, 2^i$$

In such a representation the largest negative value is the same as the largest positive value. The sign-modulus representation has two disadvantages, one fairly trivial and one not so trivial. Firstly, there are two different bit patterns to represent zero, 0000...00, positive zero, and, 1000...00, negative zero. Secondly, the operations of adding two numbers together and of subtracting two numbers is intrinsically different, and different electronics is required to perform each operation. For these reasons most computers use a different method of representing negative values, the most common is the so called two's complement representation.

In sign-modulus representation
+1 is   000...01
−1 is   100...01

In two's complement
+1 is   000...01
−1 is   111...11

In effect the bits could be considered like a binary version of the decade counters which count revolutions of the take-up spool on a cassette player. If this was a binary counter and not a decimal counter each wheel would have just two numbers on it, not ten. As the first wheel completes a revolution it would cause the next to rotate half a turn, and so on, counting revolutions of the take-up spool in binary. Forward revolutions then count in the positive sense, reverse revolutions count in the negative sense. Plus operations can be performed on such a device by doing the necessary number of forward revolutions, and minus operations by doing the necessary number of reverse revolutions. However, anyone who has played with the counter on a cassette player will know that there are no negative numbers as such. If the player is rewound so that the counter goes back past zero, it moves from zero to all nines in one further revolution. Our binary counter will do the totally analogous thing. It will go from all zeros to all ones for one revolution in the negative sense from zero, hence the representation above for -1. The largest negative number in two's complement, the value with only the leading bit set — all others zero, represents the value -2^{n-1}.

In two's complement there is only one representation for zero — all bits zero, and there is one more negative value than positive values; that is, the 2^n possible bit patterns are used to represent the values from -2^{n-1} to $2^{n-1}-1$.

A simple rule for constructing the two's complement representation for any value is:

(i)   Form the binary representation of the positive, absolute value of the number.

(ii)   Invert the state of each bit, replace each zero with one and each one with zero.

(iii)   Add one to the result.

For example, to represent -19 in two's complement (8 bits):

(i)   +19   = 00010011
(ii)   bit complement   = 11101100
(iii)   add 1   = 11101101 = -19

Subtraction can be done very simply in terms of binary addition using the two complement representation of the negative value. The rule is the two values are simply added using the rules of binary addition, ignoring the fact that the leading bit is actually a sign bit and also ignoring any carry which would normally be the $(n+1)^{th}$ bit of the result.

For example, take the representations for $+19$ and -19 above

$$+19 = \quad 00010011$$
$$-19 = \quad 11101101 \text{ (remember in binary addition } 1+1 = 10)$$
$$\overline{}$$
$$(1)00000000$$
$$\overline{}$$

ignoring the final carry gives 8 zero bits as expected.

$$
\begin{array}{ll}
+27 = & 00011011 \\
-19 = & 11101101 \\
\hline
+8 & (1)00001000 \\
\hline
\end{array}
$$

A further representation for negative numbers which is also used, but less commonly than two's complement, is the so called one's complement. This works on a principle that is similar to our revolving counter but it treats all zeros and all ones as alternative representations for zero, positive and negative. In this representation negative numbers are simply the bit inverses of positive numbers. In positive numbers the one bits indicate non-zero contributions to the value and in negative numbers the zero bits indicate the non-zero contributions. That is,

00....00 to 01....11 represent values from $+0$ to $+(2^{n-1}-1)$
11....11 to 10....00 represent values from -0 to $-(2^{n-1}-1)$

Subtraction is again done easily in terms of addition. In this case the two binary representatives are again simply added ignoring the significance of the sign bit, but now, if a carry off the end occurs, one must be added to the result.

$$
\begin{array}{lll}
\text{e.g.} & +27 = & 00011011 \\
& -19 = & 11101100 \\
& & \hline
& & (1)00000111 \\
& & \hline
& 8 = & 00001000 \\
\end{array}
$$

One's complement, like sign-modulus, has two distinct representations for zero and for this, among other more technical reasons, two's complement is usually preferred. Most modern computers, and certainly all major microprocessors, use two's complement representations and arithmetic for integers.

1.3 The Representation of Floating-Point Numbers

To represent non-integral values and values which are much larger or smaller than can be held conveniently in a normal word length sized string of bits, the so called 'floating-point' representation is used. This in general represents not exact values but approximate values 'correct' to a number of significant digits. The representation is analogous to the common scientific notation for large and small quantities, viz. a value such as 12345.67 in scientific notation would be written as 1.234567×10^4. That is, the values are written with a mantissa, or significand, in some defined range and with an exponent, or power, of 10. The product of the two parts gives the value.

As with integers, direct representation of numbers in a decimal form is not normally done. A radix of 2 or 16 is normally used as this codes more directly into a bit-string representation. In all cases a word is divided into two main parts. One part represents a binary or a hex exponent and the other the normalized mantissa.

If we take B to be the radix, or base, of the number system, values are represented such that

$$x = fB^e$$

where f is the normalized mantissa and e is the base B exponent.

Two normalizations are in common use

$$1/B < |f| < 1 \quad \text{or} \quad 1 < |f| < B$$

In the first, f is a pure fraction and the radix point is at the left of the mantissa; in the second, the radix point is one digit position in from the left. In both cases the normalization condition ensures that the leading digit of the mantissa is non-zero. The exact choice is of little actual significance as it simply changes the exponent value by one. Of the two normalizations the fractional normalization is the more common. It is used by all hex, $B = 16$, systems and many binary, $B = 2$, systems. But the 1 to B normalization is used by a number of very important binary systems. A very small number of systems use a normalization which makes the mantissa an integer but with a leading non-zero bit — the binary point being taken to be at the right of the mantissa.

All possible real values can be represented in this floating-point fashion but many such values do not have a finite representation. That is, they require an infinite string of digits in the mantissa to represent the exact value; for example the value $pi = 3.14159...$ An infinite string of digits, will be required in any base to represent pi. Hence, in a finite number of bits only an approximation can be represented. The mantissa must be limited to a finite number of the leading most significant digits. Similarly, very large numbers, or very small numbers, will require a large positive or negative value for the exponent. Again a limited number of bits are available to represent the exponent, hence there is a limit to the range of values that can be represented.

Floating-point representations are therefore in general characterized by four parameters:
(1)   The radix or normalization base, B
(2)   The number of base B digits retained in the mantissa, t
(3)   The largest positive exponent, E
(4)   The largest negative exponent, e

There are two bases in common use: a binary base, $B = 2$, and a hex base, $b = 16$. Other bases are possible, 4 and 8 for instance, but these are not found today on any commonly available machine. Various complicated systems for representing floating-point values with a decimal base have also been proposed, and some have even been implemented, but no commonly available system currently on the market uses a decimal base.

In terms of these four parameters, other values of significance can be calculated.
(i)   The largest representable value, HUGE $= (1 - B^{-t})B^E$.
(ii)   The smallest non-zero representable value, TINY $= B^{e-1}$.
(iii)   The maximum relative spacing between adjacent, exactly representable values, EPS $= B^{1-t}$ (this is sometimes called the relative accuracy).
(iv)   The effective decimal precision,
PRECISION $=$ INT $((t-1)\log_{10}B)$ (INT$(a) =$ largest integer less than or equal to a).
(v)   The number of effective decimal digits,
NDIG $= \lceil t \log_{10}B+1 \rceil$ ($\lceil a \rceil =$ smallest integer greater than or equal to a).
N.B. These two values are very different. The first is the maximum number of decimal digits that can be represented correctly in the floating-point system. The second is the minimum number of decimal digits that must be specified in order to obtain a floating-point approximation that is 'faithful'. An approximation is said to be faithful if no representable value lies between the approximate value and the true value.

The relative accuracy of a floating-point system is determined not only by the details of the representation format, but depends on the precise methods used to perform arithmetic. The exact result of an arithmetic operation with floating operands will normally require more bits to represent it than are available in the machine, and certainly more than can be stored in the given floating-point format. Therefore, an additional error will be introduced by the technique employed to abbreviate the result to the required length. Two main techniques are used: the first, called truncation or chopping, simply discards all digits in the mantissa in excess of the number of leading digits that can be fitted into the format; the second discards the excess digits but 'rounds' to the nearest representable value. A chopped system has a relative accuracy bounded by EPS and a rounded system bounded by EPS/2.

Virtually all systems using a hex base employ the same actual floating-point representation. All such machines are byte-based and they use 32-bit, 64-bit and, frequently for mainframe machines, 128-bit word sizes for floating-point values. Machines in this category include:

> IBM 43xx, 30xx, 308x
> ICL 29xx (VME)
> Honeywell DPS7
> Amdahl 470, 58xx
> Fujitsu
> Hitachi
> N.E.C.
> GEC 4xxx

The floating-point format has:

(a)   32-bit.
      1 sign bit, 7-bit exponent, 24-bit mantissa

$B = 16$	$\text{HUGE} = 16^{63}(1-16^{-6}) = 7.2 \times 10^{75}$
$t = 6$	$\text{TINY} = 16^{-65} = 5.4 \times 10^{-79}$
$E = 63$	$\text{EPS} = 9.5 \times 10^{-7}$
$e = -64$	$\text{PRECISION} = 6$
	$\text{NDIG} = 9$

(b)   64-bit.
      1 sign bit, 7-bit exponent, 56-bit mantisssa

$B = 16$	$\text{HUGE} = 16^{63}(1-16^{-14}) = 7.2 \times 10^{75}$
$t = 14$	$\text{TINY} = 16^{-65} = 5.4 \times 10^{-79}$
$E = 63$	$\text{EPS} = 2.2 \times 10^{-16}$
$e = -64$	$\text{PRECISION} = 15$
	$\text{NDIG} = 18$

(c)   128-bit.
      1 sign bit, 7-bit exponent, 112-bit mantissa
      (sign/exponent byte of second double word is not used)

$B = 16$ $\qquad$ HUGE $= 16^{63}(1-16^{-28}) = 7.2 \times 10^{75}$
$t = 28$ $\qquad$ TINY $= 16^{-65} = 5.4 \times 10^{-79}$
$E = 63$ $\qquad$ EPS $= 3.1 \times 10^{-33}$
$e = -64$ $\qquad$ PRECISION $= 32$
$\qquad\qquad\quad$ NDIG $= 35$

Hex systems always employ a chopping method of abbreviation.

Unfortunately there is no such uniformity of format for machines using a binary base, even among byte machines with similar word sizes. Some of the common systems employing a binary base are:

(a) 32-bit formats on VAX, Microsoft Fortran 80 and MBASIC on micros.
1 sign bit, 8-bit exponent, 24-bit mantissa

$B = 2$ $\qquad$ HUGE $= 2^{127}(1-2^{-24}) = 1.7 \times 10^{38}$
$t = 24$ $\qquad$ TINY $= 2^{-128} = 2.94 \times 10^{-39}$
$E = 127$ $\qquad$ EPS $= 2^{-23} = 1.19 \times 10^{-7}$
$e = -127$ $\qquad$ PRECISION $= 6$
$\qquad\qquad\quad$ NDIG $= 9$

N.B. (i) In all, 33 bits are represented. Since the leading bit of a normalized binary mantissa is always one, this is not actually stored but is included implicitly.
(ii) An exponent with all bits zero is taken to represent special values. If the sign bit is also zero this represents the value zero. If the sign bit is one this represents an illegal or reserved value.
(iii) Arithmetic operations are performed with correct rounding so the relative accuracy is EPS/2 $= 5.96 \times 10^{-8}$ or an effective arithmetic precision of 7 decimal digits.
(iv) The value of NDIG is, in practice, dependent on the correctness of the software. The theoretical value of 9 is correct for the VAX, but on some micros, because of defects in the decimal to binary conversion software, a value of 8 is in fact preferable and results in representation errors for values converted from the decimal of 1.2×10^{-7} instead of the theoretically possible 6.0×10^{-8}.

(b) 64-bit format on VAX, Microsoft Fortran 80 and MBASIC on micros.
1 sign bit, 8-bit exponent, 56-bit mantissa

$$B = 2 \qquad \text{HUGE} = 2^{127}(1 - 2^{-56}) = 1.7 \times 10^{38}$$
$$t = 56 \qquad \text{TINY} = 2^{-128} = 2.94 \times 10^{-39}$$
$$E = 127 \qquad \text{EPS} = 2^{-55} = 2.78 \times 10^{-17}$$
$$e = -127 \qquad \text{PRECISION} = 16$$
$$\text{NDIG} = 18$$

N.B. (i) Implicit leading bit is again used.

(ii) Arithmetic is performed rounded, thus the relative accuracy of the system is 1.39×10^{-17}.

(c) Alternative 64-bit and 128-bit formats on the VAX.
1 sign bit, 11 bit-exponent, 53-bit mantissa

$$B = 2 \qquad \text{HUGE} = 2^{1023}(1 - 2^{-53}) = 8.98 \times 10^{307}$$
$$t = 53 \qquad \text{TINY} = 2^{-1024} = 5.6 \times 10^{-309}$$
$$E = 1023 \qquad \text{EPS} = 2^{-52} = 2.22 \times 10^{-16}$$
$$e = -1023 \qquad \text{PRECISION} = 15$$
$$\text{NDIG} = 17$$

1 sign bit, 15-bit exponent, 113-bit mantissa

$$B = 2 \qquad \text{HUGE} = 2^{16383}(1 - 2^{-113}) = 5.9 \times 10^{4931}$$
$$t = 113 \qquad \text{TINY} = 2^{-16383} = 8.4 \times 10^{-4933}$$
$$E = 16383 \qquad \text{EPS} = 2^{-112} = 1.93 \times 10^{-34}$$
$$e = -16383 \qquad \text{PRECISION} = 33$$
$$\text{NDIG} = 36$$

N.B. In both cases arithmetic is rounded and hence the relative accuracies are 1.11×10^{-16} and 0.96×10^{-34} respectively.

The IEEE has recently produced a standard for floating-point arithmetic (Ref. IEEE P754/82−8.6) based on 32- and 64-bit formats. This standard has been implemented in hardware for use in microcomputers. The Intel 8087, 80287 and Motorola 68341 implement this standard.

The IEEE format basically uses a leading sign bit, an exponent field, and the remaining bits form a binary fraction. Values are usually normalized and the leading one bit is not stored. The implicit first bit is considered to be to the left of the binary point.

(a) 32-bit format
1 sign bit, 8-bit exponent, 24-bit mantissa

$B = 2$ 1   8   23

S	r	f

$t = 24$

$E = 127$

$e = -126$

r is treated as an 8-bit positive integer value $0 < r < 255$. The values represented are then calculated as follows:

if   (1) $r = 255$ and $f \neq 0$ the value is not a number (Nan)
     (2) $r = 255$ and $f = 0$ then $v = (-1)^S$ infinity
     (3) $0 < r < 255$ then $v = (-1)^S 2^{r-127}(1.f)$
     (4) $r = 0$ and $f \neq 0$ then $v = (-1)^S 2^{-126}(0.f)$
     (5) $r = 0$ and $f = 0$ then $v = (-1)^S$ zero

This format is characterized by a range of bit patterns which are interpreted as illegal or not numbers. These are used in handling numeric errors. Two of these patterns are used to code for + and − infinity. It also has a set of denormalized values which allow a more gradual approach to underflow for very small numbers. The range of unexceptional floating-point numbers are the category (3) values

$$\text{HUGE} = 2^{127}(2 - 2^{-23}) = 3.4 \times 10^{38}$$
$$\text{TINY} = 2^{-126} = 1.18 \times 10^{-38}$$
$$\text{EPS} = 2^{-23} = 1.19 \times 10^{-7}$$
$$\text{PRECISION} = 6$$
$$\text{ND16} = 9$$

(b)   64-bit format
     1 sign bit, 11-bit exponent, 53-bit mantissa
     $B = 2$ 1   11   52

S	r	f

$t = 53$

$E = 1023$

$e = -1022$

if   (1) $r = 2047$ and $f \neq 0$ $v = \text{Nan}$

       (2) $r = 2047$ and $f = 0$ $v = (-1)^S$ infinity

       (3) $0 < r < 2047$ $v = (-1)^S 2^{r-1023}(1.f)$

       (4) $r = 0$ and $f \neq 0$ $v = (-1)^S 2^{-1022}(0.f)$

       (5) $r = 0$ and $f = 0$ $v = (-1)^S$ zero

$$\text{HUGE} = 2^{1023}(2 - 2^{-52}) = 1.79 \times 10^{308}$$
$$\text{TINY} = 2^{-1022} = 2.24 \times 10^{-308}$$
$$\text{EPS} = 2^{-52} = 2.22 \times 10^{-16}$$
$$\text{PRECISION} = 15$$
$$\text{NDIG} = 17$$

The draft standard provides a great deal more detail on arithmetic and methods of rounding, error handling, conversions, etc. The interested reader is referred to the original document for further information.

1.4   The Representation of Characters

There are two main character code systems in common use. These are ASCII (American Standard Character Information Interchange) code, and EBCDIC (Extended Binary Coded Decimal Interchange Code) codes. The former is basically a 7-bit code and, with minor variations, is also the character coding adopted by the International Standards Organization (ISO, 1A5) character codes. Most computing systems and most keyboard devices for use as computer terminals use the ASCII code. All computing systems will handle ASCII coded character devices. EBCDIC is an 8-bit code defined by IBM and used by them and a number of other mainframe manufacturers.

1.4.1 ASCII Character Codes

Octal code	Decimal code	Hex code	Characters	Control keys (see note below)	Description
000	0	0	NUL	@	Null
001	1	1	SOH	A	Start of heading
002	2	2	STX	B	Start of text
003	3	3	ETX	C	End of text
004	4	4	EOT	D	End of transmission
005	5	5	ENQ	E	Enquiry; also WRU
006	6	6	ACK	F	Acknowledge; also RU

Octal code	Decimal code	Hex code	Characters	Control keys (see note below)	Description
007	7	7	BEL	G	Rings the bell
010	8	8	BS	H	Backspace; also FEB, format effector backspace
011	9	9	HT	I	Horizontal tab
012	10	A	LF	J	Line feed: advances cursor to next line
013	11	B	VT	K	Vertical tab (VTAB)
014	12	C	FF	L	Form feed to top of next page
015	13	D	CR	M	Carriage return to beginning of line
016	14	E	SO	N	Shift out
017	15	F	SI	O	Shift in
020	16	10	DLE	P	Data line escape
021	17	11	DC1	Q	Device control 1: turns transmitter on (XON)
022	18	12	DC2	R	Device control 2
023	19	13	DC3	S	Device control 3: turns transmitter off (XOFF)
024	20	14	DC4	T	Device control 4
025	21	15	NAK	U	Negative acknowledge: also ERR (error)
026	22	16	SYN	V	Synchronous idle (SYNC)
027	23	17	ETB	W	End of transmission block
030	24	18	CAN	X	Cancel (CANCL): cancels current escape sequence
031	25	19	EM	Y	End of medium
032	26	1A	SUB	Z	Substitute
033	27	1B	ESC	[	Escape
034	28	1C	FS	\	File separator
035	29	1D	GS	]	Group separator
036	30	1E	RS	∧	Record separator
037	31	1F	US	-	Unit separator

N.B. The control codes are generated from the normal terminal keyboard by hitting the indicated key while holding down the control key, usually marked CNTL or CTRL. Most keyboards will also generate certain of these codes directly, for instance keys such as

RETURN	CR
TAB	HT
Line feed	LF
Backspace	BS
Escape	ESC

are commonly available.

Chapter 1

The description of these control character codes is as per the standard. The effect on any computer if it receives these codes is dependent on the software and the interpretation of these codes which it implements, e.g. a CNTL/C (ETX) character is used by many systems to stop a currently running process.

Octal code	Decimal code	Hex code	Characters	Description
040	32	20	SP	Space
041	33	21	!	Exclamation point
042	34	22	"	Quotation mark
043	35	23	# or £	Hash or pound
044	36	24	$	Dollar sign
045	37	25	%	Percent sign
046	38	26	&	Ampersand
047	39	27	' or ´	Acute accent or apostrophe
050	40	28	(	Open parenthesis
051	41	29	)	Close parenthesis
052	42	2A	*	Asterisk
053	43	2B	+	Plus sign
054	44	2C	,	Comma
055	45	2D	−	Hyphen or minus
056	46	2E	.	Period
057	47	2F	/	Slash
060	48	30	0	Digit 0
061	49	31	1	Digit 1
062	50	32	2	Digit 2
063	51	33	3	Digit 3
064	52	34	4	Digit 4
065	53	35	5	Digit 5
066	54	36	6	Digit 6
067	55	37	7	Digit 7
070	56	38	8	Digit 8
071	57	39	9	Digit 9
072	58	3A	:	Colon
073	59	3B	;	Semicolon
074	60	3C	<	Less than
075	61	3D	=	Equal sign
076	62	3E	>	Greater than
077	63	3F	?	Question mark
100	64	40	@	At sign
101	65	41	A	Letter A
102	66	42	B	Letter B
103	67	43	C	Letter C
104	68	44	D	Letter D
105	69	45	E	Letter E
106	70	46	F	Letter F
107	71	47	G	Letter G
110	72	48	H	Letter H
111	73	49	I	Letter I

Octal code	Decimal code	Hex code	Characters	Description
112	74	4A	J	Letter J
113	75	4B	K	Letter K
114	76	4C	L	Letter L
115	77	4D	M	Letter M
116	78	4E	N	Letter N
117	79	4F	O	Letter O
120	80	50	P	Letter P
121	81	51	Q	Letter Q
122	82	52	R	Letter R
123	83	53	S	Letter S
124	84	54	T	Letter T
125	85	55	U	Letter U
126	86	56	V	Letter V
127	87	57	W	Letter W
130	88	58	X	Letter X
131	89	59	Y	Letter Y
132	90	5A	Z	Letter Z
133	91	5B	[	Open bracket
134	92	5C	\	Reverse slash
135	93	5D	]	Close bracket
136	94	5E	^	Up arrow/caret
137	95	5F	_	Underscore
140	96	60	`	Grave accent
141	97	61	a	Letter a
142	98	62	b	Letter b
143	99	63	c	Letter c
144	100	64	d	Letter d
145	101	65	e	Letter e
146	102	66	f	Letter f
147	103	66	g	Letter g
150	104	68	h	Letter h
151	105	69	i	Letter i
152	106	6A	j	Letter j
153	107	6B	k	Letter k
154	108	6C	l	Letter l
155	109	6D	m	Letter m
156	110	6E	n	Letter n
157	111	6F	o	Letter o
160	112	70	p	Letter p
161	113	71	q	Letter q
162	114	72	r	Letter r
163	115	73	s	Letter s
164	116	74	t	Letter t
165	117	75	u	Letter u
166	118	76	v	Letter v
167	119	77	w	Letter w
170	120	78	x	Letter x

Chapter 1

Octal code	Decimal code	Hex code	Characters	Description
171	121	79	y	Letter y
172	122	7A	z	Letter z
173	123	7B	{	Left brace
174	124	7C	¦ or ǀ	Vertical bar (broken or full)
175	125	7D	}	Right brace
176	126	7E	~ or ⌐	Tilde or NOT
177	127	7F	DEL	Delete (rubout)

1.4.2 EBCDIC Character Codes

EBCDIC is a less well defined character code system than ASCII/IA5. Although there is general agreement as to coding of letters, digits and the more common special characters, there is wide variation with most of the other possible codes. This variation applies between manufacturers who claim to be using EBCDIC and even for different devices from the same manufacturer. The confusion is evident from the following table. Many of the possible 256 codes have no defined interpretation; other characters have more than one code associated with the same graphic character. In these cases of non-uniqueness, which code should be used is a function of the peripheral device. Where there is this duplication one version is shown in bold type. This is the code which is used in the IBM standard version and this is the code used with most software requiring the use of this character. The alternatives are known to be those used by certain peripheral devices employing EBCDIC codes.

Decimal code	Hex code	Characters (controls)	Description
0	0	NUL	Null
1	1	SOH	Start of heading
2	2	STX	Start of text
3	3	ETX	End of text
4	4	SEL	
5	5	HT	Horizontal tab
6	6	RNL	
7	7	DEL	Delete
8	8	GE	
9	9	SPS	

Decimal code	Hex code	Characters (controls)	Description
10	A	RPT	
11	B	VT	Vertical tab
12	C	FF	Form feed
13	D	CR	Carriage return
14	E	SO	Shift out
15	F	SI	Shift in
16	10	DLE	Data line escape
17	11	DC1	Device control 1
18	12	DC2	Device control 2
19	13	DC3	Device control 3
20	14	RES/ENP	
21	15	NL	New line
22	16	BS	Back space
23	17	POC	
24	18	CAN	Cancel
25	19	EM	End of medium
26	1A	UBS	
27	1B	CU1	
28	1C	IFS	
29	1D	IGS	
30	1E	IRS	
31	1F	ITB/IUS	
32	20	DS	
33	21	SOS	
34	22	FS	
35	23	WUS	
36	24	BYP/INP	
37	25	LF	Line feed
38	26	ETB	End transmission block
39	27	ESC	Escape
40	28	SA	
41	29	SFE	
42	2A	SM/SW	
43	2B	CSP	
44	2C	MFA	
45	2D	ENQ	Enquiry
46	2E	ACK	Acknowledge
47	2F	BEL	Sound bell
48	30	-	
49	31	-	
50	32	SYN	
51	33	IR	
52	34	PP	
53	35	TRN	
54	36	NBS	
55	37	EOT	
56	38	SBS	
57	39	IT	

Decimal code	Hex code	Characters (controls)	Description
58	3A	RFF	
59	3B	CU3	
60	3C	DC4	
61	3D	NAK	Negative acknowledge
62	3E	-	
63	3F	USB	
64	40	SP	Space/blank
65	41		
66	42		
67	43		
68	44		
69	45		
70	46		
71	47		
72	48		
73	49		
74	4A	¢	Cent/currency
75	4B	.	Period
76	4C	<	Less than
77	4D	(	**Left parenthesis**
78	4E	+	**Plus**
79	4F	|	**Vertical line**
80	50	&	Ampersand
81	51		
82	52		
83	53		
84	54		
85	55		
86	56		
87	57		
88	58		
89	59		
90	5A	!	Exclamation
91	5B	$	Dollar
92	5C	*	Asterisk
93	5D	)	**Right parenthesis**
94	5E	;	Semi-colon
95	5F	¬	Logical not
96	60	−	**Minus**
97	61	/	Slash
98	62		
99	63		
100	64		
101	65		
102	66		
103	67		
104	68		
105	69		

Decimal code	Hex code	Characters (controls)	Description
106	6A	¦	Broken vertical line
107	6B	,	Comma
108	6C	%	Percent
109	6D	_	Underscore
110	6E	>	Greater than
111	6F	?	Query
112	70		
113	71	∧ or ↑	Caret or up arrow
114	72		
115	73		
116	74		
117	75		
118	76		
119	77		
120	78		
121	79	`	Grave
122	7A	:	Colon
123	7B	# or £	Hash or pound
124	7C	@	At
125	7D	'	Apostrophe
126	7E	=	Equals
127	7F	"	Quote
128	80		
129	81	a	Small a
130	82	b	Small b
131	83	c	Small c
132	84	d	Small d
133	85	e	Small e
134	86	f	Small f
135	87	g	Small g
136	88	h	Small h
137	89	i	Small i
138	8A		
139	8B	{	Left brace
140	8C	≤	**Less than or equal to**
141	8D	(	Left parenthesis
142	8E	+	Plus
143	8F	†	Dagger
144	90		
145	91	j	Small j
146	92	k	Small k
147	93	l	Small l
148	94	m	Small m
149	95	n	Small n
150	96	o	Small o
151	97	p	Small p
152	98	q	Small q
153	99	r	Small r

Decimal code	Hex code	Characters (controls)	Description
154	9A		
155	9B	}	Right brace
156	9C	□	Open box
157	9D	)	Right parenthesis
158	9E	±	**Plus/minus**
159	9F	■	Filled box
160	A0	─	Minus
161	A1	°	Degree sign
162	A2	s	Small s
163	A3	t	Small t
164	A4	u	Small u
165	A5	v	Small v
166	A6	w	Small w
167	A7	x	Small x
168	A8	y	Small y
169	A9	z	Small z
170	AA		
171	AB	└	Lower left corner
172	AC	┌	Upper left corner
173	AD	[	Left bracket
174	AE	≥	**Greater than or equal to**
175	AF	●	Bullet
176	B0	^{0}	Superscript zero
177	B1	^{1}	Superscript 1
178	B2	^{2}	Superscript 2
179	B3	^{3}	Superscript 3
180	B4	^{4}	Superscript 4
181	B5	^{5}	Superscript 5
182	B6	^{6}	Superscript 6
183	B7	^{7}	Superscript 7
184	B8	^{8}	Superscript 8
185	B9	^{9}	Superscript 9
186	BA		
187	BB	┘	Lower right corner
188	BC	┐	Upper right corner
189	BD	]	Right bracket
190	BE	≠	**Not equal to**
191	BF	─	Minus
192	C0	{	**Left brace**
193	C1	A	Capital A
194	C2	B	Capital B
195	C3	C	Capital C
196	C4	D	Capital D
197	C5	E	Capital E
198	C6	F	Capital F
199	C7	G	Capital G
200	C8	H	Capital H
201	C9	I	Capital I

Decimal code	Hex code	Characters (controls)	Description
202	CA		
203	CB		
204	CC		
205	CD		
206	CE		
207	CF		
208	D0	}	**Right brace**
209	D1	J	Capital J
210	D2	K	Capital K
211	F3	L	Capital L
212	D4	M	Capital M
213	D5	N	Capital N
214	D6	O	Capital O
215	D7	P	Capital P
216	D8	Q	Capital Q
217	D9	R	Capital R
218	DA		
219	DB		
220	DC		
221	DD		
222	DE		
223	DF		
224	EO	\	Back slash
225	E1		
226	E2	S	Capital S
227	E3	T	Capital T
228	E4	U	Capital U
229	E5	V	Capital V
230	E6	W	Capital W
231	E7	X	Capital X
232	E8	Y	Capital Y
233	E9	Z	Capital Z
234	EA		
235	EB		
236	EC		
237	ED		
238	EE		
239	EF		
240	F0	0	Digit 0
241	F1	1	Digit 1
242	F2	2	Digit 2
243	F3	3	Digit 3
244	F4	4	Digit 4
245	F5	5	Digit 5
246	F6	6	Digit 6
247	F7	7	Digit 7
248	F8	8	Digit 8
249	F9	9	Digit 9

Decimal code	Hex code	Characters (controls)	Description
250	FA	|	Vertical line
251	FB		
252	FC		
253	FD		
254	FE		
255	FF	EO	Control code

1.4.3 ASCII/IA5 to EBCDIC Translation

There is no fully standard translation of ASCII to a subset of EBCDIC. However, since ASCII is the character set used by all microcomputers and most terminals and printers, a translation is necessary. This need is made even more pressing by the advent of networks linking more than one type of computing system. In the UK the Data Communications Protocol Unit, as part of the definition of a 'Network Independent File Transfer Protocol' (Blue Book), have proposed a general subset of EBCDIC and such a standard translation table. The subset includes all the control codes from EBCDIC which have a correspondence in ASCII/IA5 and all the 'printable' characters commonly used in software. The following table gives the translation from ASCII/IA5 to EBCDIC and vice versa.

N.B. The common ASCII graphic for code 7C is a broken vertical line. This is normally interpreted by software as the logical disjunction, OR, and so is mapped to the EBCDIC, 4F, the unbroken vertical line used for the same purpose. Similarly, the ASCII code 7E for tilde is mapped to EBCDIC, 5F, the logical NOT symbol, since these are both common software interpretations of both these characters. Apart from these two 'mis-matches' the ASCII and EBCDIC graphics are conventionally the same for this mapping. EBCDIC codes outside this subset do not have a mapping into ASCII.

ASCII/EBCDIC Character	ASCII/IA5 Hex code	EBCDIC Hex code
NUL	00	00
SOH	01	01
STX	02	02
ETX	03	03
EOT	04	37
ENQ	05	2D
ACK	06	2F
BEL	07	2F
BS	08	16
HT	09	05
LF	0A	25
VT	0B	0B
FF	0C	0C
CR	0D	0D
SO	0E	0E
SI	0F	0F
DLE	10	10
DC1	11	11
DC2	12	12
DC3	13	13
DC4	14	14
NAK	15	3D
SYN	16	32
ETB	17	26
CAN	18	18
EM	19	19
SUB	1A	3F
ESC	1B	27
FS/IFS	1C	1C
GS/IGS	1D	1D
RS/IRS	1E	1E
US/IUS	1F	1F
Space	20	40
!	21	5A
"	22	7F
#	23	7B
$	24	5B
%	25	6C
&	26	50
'	27	7D
(	28	4D
)	29	5D
*	2A	5C
+	2B	4E
,	2C	6B

ASCII/EBCDIC Character	ASCII/IA5 Hex code	EBCDIC Hex code
−	2D	6O
.	2E	4B
/	2F	61
0	30	F0
1	31	F1
2	32	F2
3	33	F3
4	34	F4
5	35	F5
6	36	F6
7	37	F7
8	38	F8
9	39	F9
:	3A	7A
;	3B	5E
<	3C	4C
=	3D	7E
>	3E	6E
?	3F	6F
@	40	7C
A	41	C1
B	42	C2
C	43	C3
D	44	C4
E	45	C5
F	46	C6
G	47	C7
H	48	C8
I	49	C9
J	4A	D1
K	4B	D2
L	4C	D3
M	4D	D4
N	4E	D5
O	4F	D6
P	50	D7
Q	51	D8
R	52	D9
S	53	E2
T	54	E3
U	55	E4
V	56	E5
W	57	E6
X	58	E7
Y	59	E8

ASCII/EBCDIC Character	ASCII/IA5 Hex code	EBCDIC Hex code
Z	5A	E9
[	5B	AD
\	5C	EO
]	5D	BD
∧	5E	71
−	5F	6D
`	60	79
a	61	81
b	62	82
c	63	83
d	64	84
e	65	85
f	66	86
g	67	87
h	68	88
i	69	89
j	6A	91
k	6B	92
l	6C	93
m	6D	94
n	6E	95
o	6F	96
p	70	97
q	71	98
r	72	99
s	73	A2
t	74	A3
u	75	A4
v	76	A5
w	77	A6
x	78	A7
y	79	A8
z	7A	A9
{	7B	CO
| or ¦	7C	4F
}	7D	DO
~ or ⌐	7E	5F
DEL	7F	07

1.5   Language Support for Fundamental Data Types

Most high-level computer languages provide support for manipulating data objects whose representation in the machine is in terms of one or other of the types of coding summarized in this chapter. The procedural languages, such as BASIC, Fortran, Pascal, Algol 60, Algol 68, C, Ada, APL and many others, all provide facilities for the manipulation of integers and floating-point values (usually called REAL values). Most have facilities for manipulating character-valued data or strings of characters. They also allow the manipulation of logical or Boolean, true/false values, and some provide for the use of actual bit strings. All these languages have facilities, of greater or lesser sophistication for working with homogeneous sequences of data of these types, called arrays. Some, most notably Pascal, Algol 68, and Ada, allow the definition and manipulation of heterogeneous groups of data of different fundamental types.

In all these languages, the fundamental types of data supported by the language facilities are mapped onto the data representations covered in this chapter. The specific details of this mapping on any particular computing system, for any particular language, must be gleaned from the appropriate system and/or language manuals. The variations are too numerous to be covered in a summary book of this nature. However, it is hoped that the information included in this chapter will help in providing general guidance as to the likely mappings.

Chapter Two
Chips

Chips are integrated circuits. That is, a chip is a packaged solid state semiconductor device containing a large set of transistors and other components interconnected on a small silicon wafer.

The most common package is a plastic or ceramic dual in line (DIL). It has rows of pins along two sides of the package. The total number of pins depends upon usage and ranges from 14 to 64.

Chips with higher complexity and scale of integration require more external connections, which can be achieved using pins on four sides of the chip package or using a similar, but pinless, chip carrier. This is a ceramic package with connections brought out to the edges but not standing proud of them. These chips are directly soldered to printed circuit boards or ceramic substrates.

The technology for fabrication of digital integrated circuits divides into two main types:

(a) Bipolar, based on P and N type transistors.

(b) MOS (Metal Oxide Semiconductor), based on field effect transistors (FET).

The bipolar type is distinguished by the interconnection details to the chip which may be transistor-transistor logic (TTL), emitter-coupled logic (ECL), or integrated injection logic (I^2L).

The MOS type is available in PMOS (original type) and NMOS, also CMOS which is a combination of N and P type FETs (C is for complementary).

The different fabrication technologies result in different properties for the chips.

(a) Bipolar are faster than MOS. Both PMOS and NMOS are slightly faster than CMOS.

(b) Bipolar consumes much more power than MOS. The CMOS type consumes the least power.

(c) Bipolar integration is lower than MOS type.

(d) MOS types are very susceptible to static electricity during handling because of their high impedance inputs. Most devices include internal diodes for protection, but care is required when handling these devices.

(e)   Bipolar and PMOS types may require several voltage levels for operation. However, CMOS and NMOS operate on a single +5V supply.

Typical operating voltages for bipolar devices are V_{CC} = +5 volts and the ground potential GND = 0 volts. The NMOS devices have V_{CC} = +5 volts and V_{SS} = 0 volts; CMOS have V_{DD} = +ve and V_{SS} = zero or −ve. CMOS can operate over a wide voltage range, typically 3 volts to 18 volts.

2.1   Packages

The pins of DIL packages are numbered from the left hand corner near the spot, in an anticlockwise direction when viewed from above. Figure 2.1 illustrates the pin layout for a 16-pin DIL package.

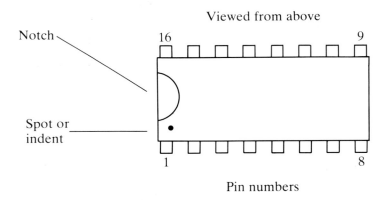

Fig. 2.1.

The package will be marked with the device type, date of manufacture and maker's logo. The device type is usually numeric and prefixed by manufacturer's code letters. Suffixes give usage information.

The date is a numeric code giving year and either month or week of manufacture, or a batch number.

Table 2.1 gives common prefix letters used for different device types.

Table 2.1. Prefix codes.

Manufacturers	Logic I.C.	Microcomputers		
		4-bit	8-bit	16-bit
Advanced Micro Devices	–	Am	Am	Am
American Microsystems	–	S	S	S
Fairchild	μA	–	F	F
Ferranti	–	–	–	F
Fujitsu	–	–	MBL	–
Hitachi	–	HM	HD	HD
Matsushita	–	MN	–	–
Mostek	–	–	MK	MK
Motorola	MC	MC	MC	MC
Mullard	FJ	–	MA	–
National	LM	IDM	INS/NS	NS
NEC	–	μPD	μPD	–
Plessey	SL	–	–	–
RCA	CD	–	CD	–
Rockwell	–	MM	R	R
Texas	SN	TMS	TMS	TMS
Zilog	–	–	Z	Z

Table 2.2 gives suffix letters for integrated circuit identification numbers.

Table 2.2. Suffix codes.

Suffix	Remarks
A	Version type of microprocessor
AE	0–15V supply, logic I.C.
BE	0–18V supply, logic I.C.
C	CMOS type
E	Microprocessor requiring external clock, microprocessor with EPROM
F	Ceramic DIL
K	Ceramic flat pack
N	Plastic DIL, logic I.C.
P	Plastic DIL
Q	Plastic quad-in line

Handling integrated circuits

No special precautions are required for TTL devices.

CMOS devices may be easily damaged by static although many devices do have built-in protection diodes fitted to the input pins. Most CMOS devices are stored in a conductive foam or a conductive package lined with silver paper or metal to ensure the minimum potential difference between the pins. Try to avoid handling the pins of CMOS devices and leave them in their packaging until required.

2.2   Logic I.C.s

Table 2.3 shows the standard convention adopted for TTL (transistor-transistor logic) and compatible MOS devices — that of 'positive true' notation.

Table 2.3. Positive true logic.

Voltage level	Description
+5	TRUE = VALID = HIGH = LOGIC 1
0	FALSE = INVALID = LOW = LOGIC 0

Logic integrated circuits became available first as TTL chips in the 74 series. Table 2.4 gives some examples.

Table 2.4. Selected logic chips.

Identification code	Type	Description	Number of pins on chip
7400	TTL	Quad 2-input NAND gate	14
7402	TTL	Quad 2-input NOR gate	14
7408	TTL	Quad 2-input AND gate	14
7410	TTL	Triple 3-input NAND gate	14
7411	TTL	Triple 3-input AND gate	14
7427	TTL	Triple 3-input NOR gate	14
7430	TTL	8-input NAND gate	14
7404	TTL	Hex inverter	14
7413	TTL	Dual NAND Schmitt trigger	14
7440	TTL	Dual 4-input NAND buffer	14
7473	TTL	Dual JK flip-flop	14
7483	TTL	4-bit full adder	14
7493	TTL	4-bit binary ripple counter	14
4001	CMOS	Quad 2-input NOR gate	14
4011	CMOS	Quad 2-input NAND gate	14
4081	CMOS	Quad 2-input AND gate	14
4023	CMOS	Triple 3-input NAND gate	14
4025	CMOS	Triple 3-input NOR gate	14
4073	CMOS	Triple 3-input AND gate	14
4016	CMOS	Quad switch	14
4017	CMOS	Decode counter/divider	14

2.2.1 Truth Tables

The truth tables (2.5–2.12) for the basic logic gates tabulate the results for all the possible combinations of input values. For example, using the two-input AND table (2.5), if both inputs are connected to logic 0 (or 0 volts) then the output will be 0 volts, whereas only when both inputs are connected to logic 1 (+5 volts) will the output be +5 volts.

Table 2.5 2-input AND

Inputs		Output
0	0	0
1	0	0
0	1	0
1	1	1

Table 2.6. 2-input NAND (gives the negation of the AND output).

Inputs		Output
0	0	1
1	0	1
0	1	1
1	1	0

Table 2.7. 2-input OR.

Inputs		Output
0	0	0
1	0	1
0	1	1
1	1	1

Table 2.8. 2-input NOR (gives the negation of the OR output).

Inputs		Output
0	0	1
1	0	0
0	1	0
1	1	0

Table 2.9. 2-input exclusive-OR (known as XOR or EX-OR).

Inputs		Output
0	0	0
1	0	1
0	1	1
1	1	0

Table 2.10. 2-input exclusive-NOR (gives the negation of the exclusive-OR output).

Inputs		Output
0	0	1
1	0	0
0	1	0
1	1	1

Table 2.11. 1-input NOT (also know as an inverter or inverting buffer).

Input	Output
0	1
1	0

Table 2.12. 1-input buffer.

Input	Output
0	0
1	1

Useful functions may be obtained by connecting together the two inputs of some simple gates. For example, when the two inputs of a NAND are connected together the gate will act as a NOT gate. The same is true for a NOR gate.

2.2.2 Logic Device Symbols

Different symbols are used to identify the various logic gates in electronic circuit diagrams. Notice that the British symbols differ from the International/American symbols. Table 2.13 illustrates the basic symbols.

Table 2.13. Logic symbols used in electronic circuits.

Logic operation	Mathematical notation	British symbol	International symbol
2-input AND	$A \wedge B$		
2-input NAND	$\sim(A \wedge B)$		
2-input OR	$A \vee B$		
2-input NOR	$\sim(A \vee B)$		
2-input exclusive-OR	$\sim(A \equiv B)$		
1-input NOT	$\sim A$		
1-input buffer	A		

The symbols may be extended to represent multi-input gates. Each elementary logic operation is governed by a simple rule which may be easily extended to multiple input versions. Two examples are given below with International symbols.

Table 2.14. 3-input AND.

Inputs			Output
0	0	0	0
0	0	1	0
0	1	0	0
1	0	0	0
0	1	1	0
1	0	1	0
1	1	0	0
1	1	1	1

Table 2.15. 3-input Exclusive Or.

Inputs			Output
0	0	0	0
0	0	1	1
0	1	0	1
1	0	0	1
0	1	1	1
1	0	1	1
1	1	0	1
1	1	1	0

Details of the logic integrated circuits are often presented in terms of symbolic logic gates. Refer to the sales catalogues of electronic component suppliers for a full range of diagrams. One example, for the 4011 Quad 2-input NAND gate, is given in Fig. 2.2.

2.2.3 Half Adder and Full Adder

A half adder is a basic logic circuit which adds the bits (logic levels) on two inputs and produces two outputs, one of which is the sum of the input bits and the other is a carry bit. It is not a circuit used frequently except as a part of a full adder. The logic gate representation is given in Fig. 2.3.

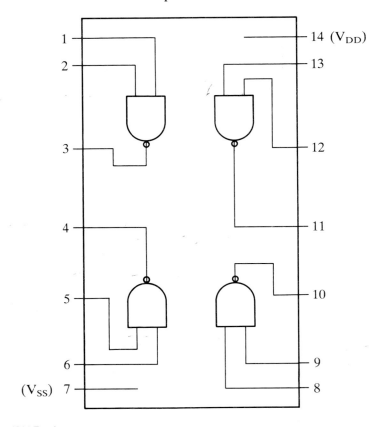

Fig. 2.2. 4011 Device.

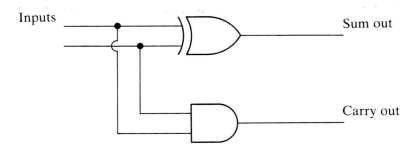

Fig. 2.3. Half adder circuit.

Table 2.16. Half adder truth table.

Inputs		Outputs	
		Sum	Carry
0	0	0	0
0	1	1	0
1	0	1	0
1	1	0	1

The half adder logic circuit is also called a two-input adder.

A more useful circuit has a similar function with three inputs and is designed to accept two inputs, as above, plus a carry bit input. It is known as a full adder and also as a three-input adder. The extra input allows a carry-in from a previous stage and means many stages may be combined to produce an adder for a large binary word input.

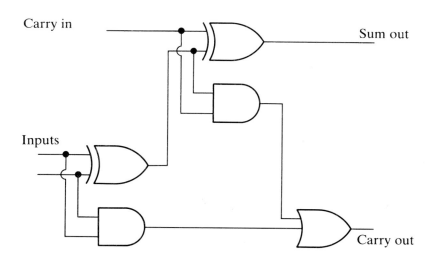

Fig. 2.4. Full adder circuit.

Table 2.17. Full adder truth table.

Inputs		Carry-in	Outputs	
			Sum	Carry-out
0	0	0	0	0
0	1	0	1	0
1	0	0	1	0
1	1	0	0	1
0	0	1	1	0
0	1	1	0	1
1	0	1	0	1
1	1	1	1	1

2.2.4 Flip-flop

A flip-flop is a basic logic device which can remain in one of the two logic states (1 or 0) until reset by an input pulse. The SET state means logic 1 output, the RESET state logic 0 output. It acts as a 1-bit storage device and is the basic constituent of registers, flags and counters. A simple reset/set known as RS flip-flop is given in Fig. 2.5.

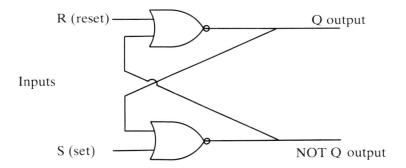

Fig. 2.5. RS flip-flop circuit.

Two outputs are available, one is always in the complementary state to the other. Often only one output is available (or used). Simultaneous input of logic 1 on R and S is forbidden.

Table 2.18. RS flip-flop truth table.

Inputs		Output
R	S	Q
0	0	X
1	0	0
0	1	1
1	1	FORBIDDEN

X = previous state (0 or 1).

A clocked version, with composite symbol, is shown in Fig. 2.6.

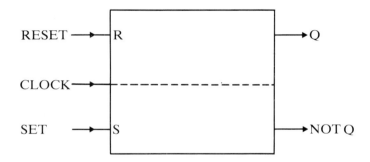

Fig. 2.6. Clocked RS flip-flop symbol.

Data must be stable on the R and S inputs when the clock pulse arrives which allows a change of state at the outputs. Many devices have two additional inputs, DC SET and DC RESET, to alter the state of the outputs regardless of the clock.

The JK flip-flop is one of the most widely used devices and has the unique property among flip-flops of allowing both input lines to be logic 1 if required.

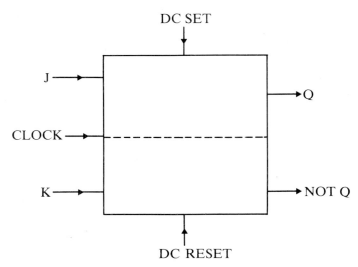

Fig. 2.7. JK flip-flop symbol.

Table 2.19. JK flip-flop truth table.

| Inputs | | Output Q | |
| | | Before | After |
J	K	clock	clock
0	0	X	X
1	0	X	1
0	1	X	0
1	1	1	0
1	1	0	1

X = previous state (0 or 1).

The last two rows show that the effect of both inputs at logic 1 is to complement (or switch) the existing state of the output Q.

2.3   Microprocessors

A complete microcomputer is fabricated from several chips which are interconnected via ancillary components and power supplies.

The central processing unit (CPU) is often called the microprocessor (μP) and usually constructed on one chip. This contains control and timing logic, arithmetic and logic unit (ALU), instruction decoder, program counter, accumulator and working registers.

Data is transferred between the chips along sets of parallel wires called buses. There are usually three buses in a complete system: one for data, one for control signals and one for addresses. In some systems one bus may carry out two or more of the above functions by being time-multiplexed. This means it may carry both data and address signals but in a pre-determined time sequence so both transmitting and receiving devices can separate the information correctly. Such a technique is sometimes used to reduce the number of pins needed on a μP chip, but it leads to more complicated logic circuitry on the chip and in external devices.

In published material, computer store sizes are quoted using the symbol K, which means the value 1024, that is 2^{10}, fairly consistently, but use the symbol M, which means the value $(1024)^2$, that is 2^{20}, only when referring to addressing ranges. Otherwise M refers to 1000K.

2.3.1 Types of Processors

Small, virtually complete, computers are available which are fabricated on a single chip. They are designed for controlling domestic appliances, computer games and routine applications which use a small pre-set program stored in the ROM on the chip.

Many μP chips are available which handle a variety of word lengths. Generally the fewer bits in a word the less complex the logic circuitry required. So 4-bit word devices were the first μP chips, followed by a large number of 8-bit word devices. A smaller group of 16-bit word devices are now available and a few 32-bit word devices are coming into general use.

Bit-slice processors implement all the CPU functions for a fixed number of bits (for example, 4-bit words) but may be linked together in parallel so that they can make up the functions of a larger word processor. Such composite computers require the definition of an assembly language set of instructions to drive the system. This assembly language is defined in terms of microcode which instructs the lowest level elements of the bit slice chips to work together.

2.4   8-bit Processors

Table 2.20 outlines the physical characteristics of the μPs dealt with in this section. Architectural comments and support chips are given in the following sections.

Table 2.20. Popular 8-bit microprocessors.

	MOS Technology 6502	Motorola 6800	Intel 8080	8085	Zilog Z80
Package	40 DIL	40 DIL	40 DIL	40 DIL	40 DIL
Max. power	800 mW	500 mW	800 mW	850 mW	1000 mW
Voltage	OV pin 1,21 +5V pin 8	OV pin 1,21 +5V pin 8	OV pin 2 +5V pin 20 −5V pin 11 +12V pin 28	OV pin 20 +5V pin 40	OV pin 29 +5V pin 11
Reset	pin 40 (low)	pin 40 (low)	pin 12 (high)	pin 36 (low)	pin 26 (low)
Data bus	pins 33–26	pins 33–26	pins 10–7, 3–6	pins 12–19 (see below)	pins 14,15, 12,8,7,9, 10,13
Address bus	pins 9–20, 22–25	pins 9–20, 22–25	pins 25–27, 29–35,1,40, 37–39,36	pins 12–19, 21–28	pins 30–40, 1–5
Clock	pins 3,37	pins 3,37	pins 22,15	pins 1,2	pin 6
Speeds	1 MHz 2 MHz-A 3 MHz-B	1 MHz 1.5 MHz-A 2 MHz-B	2 MHz 3 MHz-A1 2.6 MHz-A2	3 MHz 5 MHz-A2	2.5 MHz 4 MHz-A

N.B. (i) The 6502 and 6800 share many external characteristics but are not equivalent.

(ii) Both data and address buses are given in increasing order from the least significant bit, designated usually AØ or DØ. The 8085 multiplexes the data bus with the lower part of the address bus.

(iii) The speeds are followed by a code number or letter indicating the appropriate chip type. Thus the 6502A runs at 2 MHz.

(iv) Most of the popular μP chips described above are manufactured under licence by other manufacturers and issued with different code numbers. Table 2.21 gives the direct equivalences.

Table 2.21. Equivalents for 8-bit processors.

Type	Equivalents
6502	Rockwell R6502, EMM-Semi 6502, Synertek SY6502
6800	American Microsystems S6800, Fairchild F6800, Hitachi HD46800D, Thomson EF6800
8080	Advanced Micro Devices Am8080A, Am9080, National INS8080A, N.E.C. μPD8080A, Texas Instruments TMS8080A, Toshiba TMP8080A, Mitsubishi MSL8080A, Siemens SAB8080A
8085	Advanced Micro Devices Am8085A, Siemens SAB8085, National INS8085A, N.E.C. μPD8085A, Toshiba TMP8085A, Mitsubishi MSL8085A
Z80	N.E.C. μPD780C, μPD780C-1, Mostek MK3880, MK3880A

2.4.1 6502 Family

The MOS 6502 made by MOS Technology is one of the most commonly used μP chips for home computers and small business systems. It has had a long life beginning with the first Commodore PET computers, being used in Apple computers, and still appearing in the BBC computer, and many others.

The 6502 is an NMOS 8-bit CPU with 8-bit wide internal registers, including the accumulator which is used for arithmetic computations. It has a 16-bit wide program counter so may address 64K of memory.

The 6502's instruction set is superficially similar to that of the 6800, and it may use some 6800 support devices. Table 2.22 gives some of the family of 6502 devices.

Table 2.22. Selected 6502 support devices.

Device	Action
6520	Two 8-bit bidirectional programmable ports
6522	Versatile interface adaptor
6541	Keyboard/display controller
6545	CRT display controller
6551	Asynchronous serial I/O
6591	Floppy disk controller

2.4.2 6800 Family

The MC6800 made by Motorola is a well designed, easy-to-use and popular μP chip. It is an 8-bit NMOS CPU with three 16-bit wide registers including the program counter, and a dual 8-bit wide accumulator which speeds up arithmetic computations. It may use external memory locations as general purpose registers. The input and output are memory mapped, which means they appear as memory locations to the CPU and are accessed as other memory locations.

Table 2.23 gives some of the family of 6800 devices.

Table 2.23. Selected 6800 support devices.

Device	Action
6820, 6821	Peripheral interface adaptors
6844	Direct memory access controller
6843, 6849	Floppy disk controllers
6845, 6847	Display controllers
6850	Communications interface (Asynchronous)
6852	Serial interface

2.4.3 8080 and 8085 Families

As the Intel 8080 was the first powerful 8-bit μP it has a few design shortcomings which were remedied in the other CPUs. For example, multiple voltage supplies are required and the clock signals are quite complex to produce. It was used in a wide range of computers, but has been largely superseded by the 8085 which has a simpler voltage supply and clock signals and other improvements. The 8085 uses all the instructions of the 8080 and has a few additional ones; however, it can use all the peripheral devices of the 8080.

Both CPUs have six 8-bit registers which dual to produce three 16-bit general purpose registers, and a 16-bit stack pointer and program counter. However, the accumulator is 8-bits wide. Extra external circuitry is needed to support the 8085 because it has the data bus multiplexed with the lower 8 bits of the address bus.

Table 2.24 gives some of the family of 8080 and 8085 devices.

Table 2.24. Selected 8080 and 8085 support devices.

Device	Action
8202	RAM controller
8212	8-bit I/O port
8224	Clock generator (8080 only)
8251	Programmable serial I/O interface
8257	Direct memory access controller
8271	Floppy disk controller
8278, 8279	Keyboard and display controllers

2.4.4 Z80 Family

The Z80 made by Zilog was designed using the 8080 as a basis. It includes amongst its instructions the whole 8080 instruction set, but has many more versatile native instructions.

The Z80 is an NMOS 8-bit CPU with four 16-bit registers, the stack pointer, the program counter and two index registers. It has two independent register sets which comprise an 8-bit accumulator and six 8-bit registers. These two sets cannot be used simultaneously but are easily switched. The Z80 is one of the most powerful 8-bit CPUs and has a wide application ranging from the Sinclair ZX80 to business computers. It is the CPU for which the well known CP/M operating system was designed.

Table 2.25 gives some of the family of Z80 devices.

Table 2.25. Selected Z80 support devices.

Device	Action
Z80-PIO (MK3881)	Parallel I/O controller
Z80-DMA (MK3883)	Direct memory access controller
Z80-SIO (MK3884)	Serial I/O controller
Z8590	Universal peripheral controller

Table 2.26. Popular 16-bit microprocessors.

	Intel		Motorola	Zilog	
	8088	8086	68000	Z8001 Z8003	Z8002 Z8004
Package	40 DIL	40 DIL	64 DIL	48 DIL	40 DIL
Max. power	1.4 W	1.4 W	1 W	1.5 W	1.5 W
Voltage	OV pin 1,20 +5V pin 40	OV pin 1,20 +5V pin 40	OV pin 16,53 +5V pin 14,49	OV pin 36 +5V pin 11	OV pin 31 +5V pin 10
Reset	21	21	18 (low)	16 (low)	14 (low)
Number of data bits	16/8	16	32/16	16	16
Data bus	pins 16–9	pins 16–2,39	pins 5–1,64–54	pins 1,38–40,43,41, 44,45,48,2–6,10,9	pins 40,32–39,1–5,9,8
Number of address bits	16+4+2	16+4+2	23	16+7	16
Address bus	pins 16–2,39–35	pins 16–2,39–35	pins 29–48,50–52	as above for Data plus pins 26,25,37,24,46,47	as above for Data
Clock	pin 19	pin 19	pin 15	pin 35	pin 30
Speeds	5 MHz	10 MHz–1 8 MHz–2 4 MHz–4	4 MHz 6 MHz–6 8 MHz–8	4 MHz	4 MHz

2.5   16-bit Processors

In 16-bit processors the packages are ceramic and the chip power dissipation is higher than the 8-bit processors. There is an amount of multiplexing between address and data buses in the smaller (40, 48) pin packages. Addresses are built up from 16 bits plus additional segment address lines in some cases. Remember that 16 bits will address 64K, 20 bits will address 1M and 23 bits will address 8M. The actual size of memory will depend on the unit chosen which is usually a byte, but if two bytes are addressed as a single unit the memory will be double (in bytes) the address size range.

Together with ancillary chips, many of the μPs described here provide virtual memory and sophisticated memory management systems.

Some of the μPs allow limited compatibility with earlier 8-bit systems from the same manufacturer. The details and architectural comments are given in the following sections.

N.B.   (i)   Both data and address buses are given in increasing order from the least significant bit (AØ and DØ). Apart from the 68000, the two buses are fully multiplexed. In addition, extra address bits are provided to increase the addressing range beyond 16 bits. These extra bits may be called segment identifiers. For the 8086 and 8088, a two-bit segment identifier is multiplexed with the first two of the top four bits of address.

(ii)   The 8088 has an external data bus 8-bits wide but internally uses 16 bits.

(iii)   The 68000 has an external data bus 16-bits wide but internally uses 32 bits.

(iv)   The Z8002 and Z8004 μPs are limited to addressing using 16 bits (64K).

2.5.1 8088 and 8086 Families

Both processors are internally compatible with the same instruction set. They also accept assembly language programs (not machine code) for the 8080 and 8085 processors.

Arithmetic is performed in 16 bits and there are four 16-bit registers which may be used also as accumulators. These may be split into pairs of 8-bit registers. Four other address (stack pointer, index) 16-bit registers are provided.

An independent bus interface contains four 16-bit pointer registers and a program counter, augmented by four 16-bit segment registers for data, stack and program addressing to produce an effective 20-bit address. The bus section and execution section work asynchronously for speed.

An 8087 processor chip is available which contains 'hardwired', a set of trigonometric functions and floating-point arithmetic. It operates as a co-processor to the 8088 and 8086 processors to give high precision, high speed arithmetic functions.

Both the 8088 and 8086 processors may use a wide range of 8080 and 8085 support chips. In addition, the 8288 bus controller and 8089 I/O processor chips are available.

2.5.2 68000 Family

The 68000 is a very powerful processor which works in 32 bits internally. It uses 23 bits to directly address 16 Mbytes (8M of 16-bit words). Many of its architectural features are more reminiscent of mainframe computers than of other microprocessors.

All internal registers are 32 bits long. There are eight general purpose registers which may act also as accumulators, seven address registers, two stack pointers (user and system) and a program counter.

Hardwired integer multiplication and division are provided by the arithmetic unit.

Input and output devices are addressed as memory in the 6800 processor, so many of the 6800 support chips can be used with the 68000. Table 2.27 gives some of the family of 68000 devices.

Table 2.27 Selected 68000 support devices.

Device	Action
68120	Peripheral controller
68230	Parallel interface
68451	Memory management unit
68560	Serial DMA interface
68341	Floating-point maths ROM
68454	Disk controller

2.5.3 Z8000 Family

This is a very powerful processor family with all its registers 16 bits long, but many of these may be divided and used as pairs of 8-bit registers, or may be combined in pairs to give 32-bit length.

A virtual management facility (using the 8010 ancillary chip) provides relocation within physical memory, data segmentation and protection. Table 2.28 shows which processors may use this function.

Table 2.28. Addressing and virtual memory with the Z8000.

	Type			
	8001	8002	8003	8004
Address bits	23	16	23	16
Range (bytes)	16M	64K	16M	64K
Virtual memory	NO	NO	YES	YES

The 16 Mbyte range is obtained by using 23 bits to address 8M 16-bit words.

The processor has sixteen 16-bit registers which may also be used as accumulators. Several are designated for index addressing and as stack pointers (user and system).

Table 2.29 gives some of the support devices for the Z8000 family.

Table 2.29. Selected Z8000 support devices.

Device	Action
8010	Memory management unit
8016	DMA controller
8030	Serial I/O
8034	Peripheral
8036	Parallel I/O

2.6 Memory Devices

The principal part of the computer memory or store is made up of random-access memory (RAM) arranged so that an address refers to a byte (8 bits) or multiple of a byte (double or quad bytes). All the RAM chips in current use depend upon cells which hold one bit (0 or 1), and are built out of transistor or capacitor elements which require a voltage to retain information. This type of memory is thus volatile.

There are two distinct types of RAM devices. In static RAM each cell contains several transistors which act as logic flip-flops and remain in a set logic state (0 or 1) until new data is entered into the cell. Because of the complexity of each cell it is only possible to place a limited number of cells onto one chip. Total chip capacity is lower than in the other type of RAM, the dynamic RAM. This has a simpler cell construction which consists of a capacitor. The charged and uncharged states of the capacitor represent the logic states. However, the charge leaks away quite quickly so that if the information is to be retained it must be read and re-written frequently. This means that every few milliseconds all the cells in a dynamic RAM must be refreshed. The refresh action may be initiated by the μP chip or ancillary memory devices, and during refresh all or part of the RAM is not available to the μP or other devices (such as peripherals). The simpler cell construction of dynamic RAMs does give a high density of cells and thus a large chip capacity.

Read-only memory (ROM) devices contain fixed data which is built into them during manufacture. They do not require any power to retain the data.

Some types of ROM may be programmed by the programmer using a special device which applies the appropriate voltages to cause links to fuse or sets gates to a permanent logic state. These are programmable read-only memory (PROM) devices. A further group allows the ROM to be re-programmed many times, a special erase action precedes each programming cycle. See Section 2.6.3.

The devices below are available from a range of manufacturers. Most use the same numeric device code with added prefix letters. The devices are made in a range of access speeds usually quoted in hundreds of nanoseconds. For example, 450 ns is 450×10^{-9} seconds.

2.6.1 Static RAM Chips

The group of chips shown in Table 2.30 are NMOS static RAM chips. The precise access time depends upon manufacturer and chip variant; a typical range is given in the table.

Table 2.30. Static RAM chips.

	RAM type		
	2102	2114	4118
Package	16 DIL	18 DIL	24 DIL
Capacity (bits)	1K	4K	8K
Organization	1024 by 1 bit	1024 by 1 bit	1024 by 1 bit
Number of address pins	10	10	10
Address (pins)	8,4–7,1,2,16–14	5–7,4–1,17–15	8–1,23,22
Data in (pins)out	11 12	14–11 14–11	9–11,13–17 9–11,13–17
Write (pin)	3 (low)	10 (low)	21 (low)
Voltage	5V pin 10 0V pin 9	5V pin 18 0V pin 9	5V pin 24 0V pin 12
Current (typical)	30mA	80mA	80mA
Access time	200–650 ns	250–450 ns	250–450 ns

Table 2.31. Static CMOS RAM Chips.

	RAM type		
	5101	6116	6264
Package	22 DIL	24 DIL	28 DIL
Capacity (bits)	1K	16K	64K
Organization	256 by 4 bits	2048 by 8 bits	8192 by 8 bits
Number of address pins	8	11	13
Address (pins)	4–1,21,5–7	8–1,23,22,19	10–3,25,24,21,23,2
Data in out	9,11,13,15 10,12,14,16	9–11,13–17 9–11,13–17	11–13,15–19 11–13,15–19
Write (pin)	20 (low)	21 (low)	27 (low)
Voltage	5V pin 22 0V pin 8	5V pin 24 0V pin 12	5V pin 28 0V pin 14
Current (typical full speed)	25mA	25mA	110mA
Access time	150–600 ns	150 ns	150 ns

The group of chips shown in Table 2.31 are CMOS static RAM chips. They have fast access time and will retain data at very low current levels (10μA) with reduced voltages (down to 2V). Thus battery support is possible to enable retention of data over a prolonged period (months).

2.6.2 Dynamic RAM Chips

The smaller capacity (and older) chips have a requirement for three voltage supplies. All the chips multiplex the address so that a row address followed by a column address is supplied to the same pins. Two pins, CAS for column address strobe input, and RAS for row address strobe input, indicate the type of address supplied. Refresh cycle time is about 2 ms.

Table 2.32. Dynamic RAM chips.

| | RAM Type | | |
	4027	4116	4164
Package	16 DIL	16 DIL	16 DIL
Capacity (bits)	4K	16K	64K
Organization	4096 by 1 bit	16384 by 1 bit	65536 by 1 bit
Number of address pins	6	7	8
Address (pins)	5,7,6,12–10	5,7,6,12–10,13	5,7,6,12–10,13,9
CAS pin	15	15	15
RAS pin	4	4	4
Data in	2	2	2
out	14	14	14
Write (pin)	3	3	3
Voltage	12V pin 8 5V pin 9 −5V pin 1 0V pin 16	12V pin 8 5V pin 9 −5V pin 1 0V pin 16	5V pin 8 0V pin 16
Current (typical)	35mA	45mA	50mA
Access time	100–250 ns	100–250 ns	150–250 ns

2.6.3 Erasable ROM Chips

All the devices described in Table 2.33 are NMOS ultra-violet erasable programmable read-only memory (EPROM) organized in 8-bit words. They operate from a single 5V supply, but require a voltage pulse of approximately 25V to program each word. A transparent lid on the chip allows the user to erase the stored bit pattern by exposing it to ultra-violet light at 253.7 nm wavelength to give a total exposure of 15 W-seconds/cm^2. Thus an ultra-violet tube with output of 10 mW/cm^2 will require 25 minutes to erase the EPROM.

The small EPROM 2758 is also known as 2508 and is a single voltage replacement for the 2708 chip which required three voltage supplies. The data and address pins are the same on the three devices.

Table 2.33. Erasable programmable ROM chips.

	EPROM Type				
	2758 2508	2716	2732	2764	27128
Package	24 DIL	24 DIL	24 DIL	28 DIL	28 DIL
Capacity (bits)	8K	16K	32K	64K	128K
Organization	1024 by 8 bits	2048 by 8 bits	4096 by 8 bits	8192 by 8 bits	16384 by 8 bits
Number of address pins	10	11	12	13	14
Address (pins)	8–1,23,22	8–1,23,22, 19	8–1,23,22, 19,21	10–3,25,24, 21,23,2	10–3,25, 24,21,23, 2,26
Data (pins)	9–11,13–17	9–11,13–17	9–11,13–17	11–13,15–19	11–13,15–19
Voltage	5V pin 24 0V pin 12	5V pin 24 0V pin 12	5V pin 24 0V pin 12	5V pin 28 0V pin 14	5V pin 28 0V pin 14
Programming pulse (pin)	21	21	20	27	27
Access time	170–450 ns	250–450 ns	250–450 ns	250 ns	250 ns

Chapter Three
Secondary Storage Media and Devices

Computers and information processing systems, such as word processors, store information in a form which is readily accessible to the system and under its direct control. The external media retain digital information, usually recorded in magnetized coatings, in large quantities for long periods of time (years).

The media used for long-term storage are magnetic tapes, magnetic disks and optical disks. However, another device, the magnetic drum, is used not for long-term storage, but as an intermediate device between magnetic disks and the very fast computer memory (store). It acts as a temporary residence for data being exchanged between disks and memory. The cache memory in some high-speed computer systems acts in a similar way.

Magnetic drum has data stored in circular tracks recorded around the cylindrical surface; it has a very high transfer rate and low capacity.

Magnetic disk has data stored in circular tracks on the surfaces of a flat circular plate. It is available in a wide range of types.

Magnetic tape has data stored along the length of the tape in tracks. It is available on open reels, in cartridges, and in cassettes with widths, ½-inch, ¼-inch, and 0.15-inch.

This chapter discusses the physical characteristics of storage media. Most operating systems and utilities provide a different logical view of the storage media to programmers via high-level languages.

Notice that a number of tape and disk formats have developed as de facto standards rather than by international agreement. Many of these units were developed in the USA and some in the UK with the result that many of the dimensions are in feet and inches rather than metric quantities. Storage capacities are quoted using the international symbols:

K = kilo = one thousand (see below)

M = mega = one million

G = giga = one thousand million = (one billion USA)

When K is used for computer store sizes it is taken to mean 1024 ($=2^{10}$), and occasionally this is the value assumed in storage media sizes in some published literature.

The other commonly used unit measure is:

bpi   meaning bits per inch.

3.1   Tape

The main magnetic tape formats are:

(a)   Open reel tape is ½-inch wide wound in lengths of 600 feet, 1200 feet, 2400 feet (most common size) and 3600 feet on spools up to 12-inch diameter (see Table 3.1). Common recording format is 9 parallel tracks along the length of the tape. One of the tracks is used as a parity check, thus 8 data bits plus parity are simultaneously recorded across the tape.

(b)   Cartridge tape is ¼-inch wide, fully enclosed in a plastic case measuring 6 inches by 4 inches approximately, containing 300 feet, 450 feet and the 600 feet of tape. Data is recorded serially on each track (from 1 to 6 tracks).

(c)   Mini cartridges are a smaller version of cartridges about the size of cassettes containing 140 feet, 300 feet and 450 feet of tape.

(d)   Cassette tape is ¼-inch wide in cases measuring 4 inches by 2½ inches approximately, very similar to the type used in domestic audio recorders. Data is recorded serially on each track.

Tape density is the recording density in bits per inch (bpi) along each track. Several different methods are used to physically represent the bits on the tape; these are:

(a)   NRZ (non return to zero). This is a format for recording binary data on tape. The magnetic recording level does not automatically change to zero after each bit. The direction of the magnetic flux codes the bits, positive for 1, negative for 0; the bits 010 could be represented as negative, positive, negative, flux levels. Also, the bits 01110 have the same flux levels, but the central positive section will be three times longer (tape recording cycles) than in the first case (Fig. 3.1).

(b)   PE (phase encoded). This is a format for recording binary data on tape which uses a magnetic flux transition to code the bits; that is the direction of the transition carries the information on whether the bit recorded is 0 or 1.

direction of the transition carries the information on whether the bit recorded is 0 or 1.

(c)   GCR (group code recording). This is a format for recording binary data on tape using the PE technique with special error checks set between data records in the group allowing higher density recording.

3.1.1 Open Reel Tape

Open reel magnetic tape has blocks of data recorded in parallel tracks along the tape separated by short gaps (see Table 3.2). The block is the unit of transfer of data between the computer and tape. The gaps allow the tape unit to stop between data blocks to await further read/write transfers from the computer. They are a fixed size for a given tape format (see Table 3.3). The size of each block is system dependent but often lies between 80 bytes (a card image) and a few kilobytes. The larger the block size the less empty space (gaps) on the tape and the more efficient is its usage. The header block is a special block at the beginning of the tape containing identification information and is system dependent.

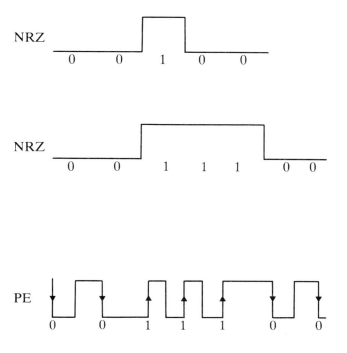

Fig. 3.1. Recording modes used for magnetic media.

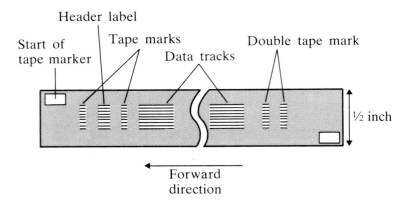

Fig. 3.2. Open reel magnetic tape.

Table 3.1. Open reel tape lengths.

Length (feet)	Reel diameter (inches)	Weight (kg)
600	7.5	0.35
1200	8.5	0.75
2400	10.5	1.00

Table 3.2. Tape characteristics.

Standard tape characteristics

Length: 600 feet, 1200 feet, 2400 feet (standard size), 3600 feet
Width: ½-inch tape
Recorded densities: 200, 556, 800, 1600, 6250 bpi
Tracks: 7 or 9
Recording mode: NRZ, PE, GCR
Interblock gap: 0.3 inches, 0.6 inches, 0.75 inches
Transfer rate is system dependent: ranges 15 to 1250 Kbytes per second
Tape speed (read/write): typically 40–200 inches per second
Tape stop/start time between blocks: typically 5–10 ms
Time to rewind a 2400 ft tape: ranges 45–120 seconds

Tape marks are on special character blocks used to identify ends of files. A double tape mark is often used to indicate the end of the last file on the tape (Fig. 3.2). The physical beginning or end of tape markers are metallic or reflective strips bonded onto the tape to indicate the permissible recording area.

Write permit rings are thin plastic rings which fit into a circular groove in the tape spool and allow data to be written to the tape. There are two types of protect rings in general use.

Table 3.3. Popular tape formats.

Generally acceptable formats	Comment
7 track 200, 556, 800 bpi NRZ Odd or even parity 0.75 inches	6 data bits plus parity bit Now largely obsolete
9 track 800 bpi NRZ Odd or even parity 0.6 inches interblock gap	IBM compatible
9 track 800, 1600 bpi PE Odd parity Interblock gap 0.6 inches	The 1600 bpi option is most common. IBM compatible
9 track 6250 bpi GCR 0.3 inches interblock gap	IBM compatible

For information retention, read and rewrite open reel tapes every 2 to 3 years, rewind to reduce 'print through' at least every 6 months.

As a measure of tape usage Table 3.4 gives examples of block sizes for a 2400 ft 9-track 1600 bpi tape using a transfer rate of 200 Kbytes per second, and interblock gap of 0.6 inches, giving a delay of 5 ms between blocks. As block sizes increase there are less interblock gaps on the tape and overall storage capacity increases.

Table 3.4. Tape capacity and data block size.

Block size (bytes)	Tape capacity (Mbytes)	Time to write 1 Mbyte (secs)
80	2.7	71
200	6.3	31
1024	20	10
4096	34	6.4
10240	39	5.6

Streamer is a name given to a microprocessor-controlled tape transport which uses the ½-inch open reel tape and operates in two modes. A low speed mode operates at 12.5 inches per second during stop/start transfer of blocks. A high speed mode operates typically at 100 inches per second for dumping or restoring large volumes of data (10s of megabytes) from disks (see Table 3.5).

Table 3.5. Tape usage on streamer transports.

Streamer type	Maximum capacity of 2400-ft reel
Standard	46 Mbytes at 1600 bpi
High capacity	92 Mbytes at 3200 bpi

3.1.2 Cartridge Tape

The original cartridge format was introduced by the 3M Corporation as the DC 300A and contained 300 feet of ¼-inch tape in a 6-inch by 4-inch plastic case — now also available in 450 feet (the DC 300 XL) and 600 feet (the DC 600A) versions.

A mini-cartridge is now also available (the DC 100A) which contains 140 feet of 0.15-inch tape.

An ANSI/ECMA standard exists for the recording format of the DC 300 range which specifies 1600 bpi, PE, 4-track serpentine layout, and block sizes from 512 bytes to 8 Kbytes. Only a minority of tape drives conform to this standard.

Tracks recorded in a serpentine manner reduce delays because rewinding is not necessary between the end of one track and the beginning of another. A 4-track serpentine layout is shown in Fig. 3.3.

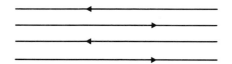

Track directions used in serpentine recording

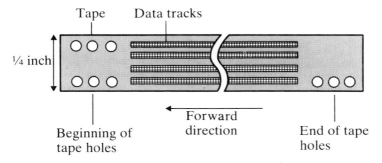

Fig. 3.3. Cartridge magnetic tape.

Many cartridge drives are used for disk backup and operate in streamer mode (see end of Section 3.1.1).

Pre-formatted cartridge tapes are also used to increase storage capacity. These formatted tapes have no interblock gaps. Formatting writes special address marks onto the tape so that the individual data blocks may be identified without the need for substantial interblock gaps. Thus more of the tape is available for data storage. The model HCD-75 drive made by 3M Corporation is an example which uses 600 ft cartridges recorded at 10 000 bpi in 16 tracks to give a usable storage capacity of 67 Mbytes (the gross capacity is 75 Mbytes which includes the pre-recorded block information).

A guide to commonly used formats and capacities for DC 300 cartridges is shown in Table 3.6. The top two rows are in ANSI/ECMA standard.

The DC 100 mini-cartridge has not an agreed recording format, a typical capacity is 100 Kbytes per track using one or two tracks on the cartridge.

Table 3.6. DC 300 cartridge formats.

Cartridge length (feet)	Tracks	Density (bpi)	Capacity (unformatted) (Mbytes)
300	4	1600	2.9
450	4	1600	4.3
300	4	6400	11.5
450	4	6400	17.3
450	4	10000	21.6

3.1.3 Cassette Tape

Two major recording formats are used. An amateur standard based on home microcomputers and using audio tape units, and a professional standard using digital recording formats. Both use the 4-inch by 2½-inch cassettes familiar to hi-fi enthusiasts containing 0.15-inch wide tape, but the digital cassettes are quality controlled to specified recording densities (bpi).

The digital cassette systems offer wide compatibility as most conform to the ISO 3047 standard. Data is recorded at 800 bpi, PE suitably blocked. The transfer rate varies with read/write speed which ranges from 2½ inches per second to 40 inches per second.

Table 3.7 gives the capacity for a 290 feet (88 metres) digital cassette tape.

Table 3.7. Digital cassette storage.

	Tracks	Density (bpi)	Capacity (Mbytes)
Unformatted	2	800	0.7
Formatted (256-byte blocks)	2	800	0.5

The audio cassette system uses a standard recorder/playback machine. Two frequencies, which are generated by the microcomputer, are used to represent the 1s and 0s. The exact frequencies depend on the type of microcomputer used. Examples are 1200 Hz for space (logic Ø) and 2400 Hz for mark (logic 1), used by the BBC microcomputer.

These frequencies, used for recording at 300 baud, are a common format which is known as the Kansas City standard. The usual audio record/playback speed of 1⅞ inches per second is used.

Table 3.8 gives tape usage for the audio system assuming the two frequencies 1200 Hz and 2400 Hz are used for space and mark.

Table 3.8. Audio cassette formats.

Data write rate (baud)	Recording action (space 1200 Hz) (mark 2400 Hz)	Effective density (bpi)
300	(space = 4 cycles) (mark = 8 cycles)	160
1200	(space = 1 cycle) (mark = 2 cycles)	640

Table 3.9 gives total unformatted capacity for cassettes identified by audio type; two tracks are recorded.

Table 3.9. Cassette storage capacity.

Type	Approximate length (feet)	Unformatted capacity (Mbytes) at		
		160 bpi	640 bpi	800 bpi
C30	150	0.07	0.29	0.36
C45	200	0.10	0.38	0.48
C60	290	0.14	0.56	0.69

3.2 Disks

Disks are manufactured in a wide variety of sizes and materials. A surface coating which retains the magnetic recording is applied to one or both sides of a thin disk made of alloy (for rigid disks) or mylar (for floppy disks). The disk diameters range from 14 inches for rigid disks down to below 3 inches for floppy disks.

The disks rotate at high speed during operation and store digital data on concentric tracks which may be accessed either by a number of fixed read/write heads or, more usually, by a single moving read/write head.

Data is recorded on disks in special fields which start with an address part containing the location of the data block in terms of the track it is on and the portion of track it occupies (Fig. 3.4). Setting up the address fields by writing the address information onto the disk is known as formatting. Each track is divided into a fixed number of equal sectors. A sector is the smallest unit of data which can be read from, or written to, a disk, and each has an address field or some means of locating (see hard-sectored floppies, Section 3.3).

Some large capacity IBM disk units offer an alternative physical format known as count, key, data (CKD), which allows variable length records to be recorded on a track. Each data area is preceded by a key and count area. The count area contains address information and the length, in bytes, of the key and data areas. The beginning of each track at the index point contains address information followed by a set of CKD records.

To increase the amount of data stored on a single disk-drive unit it is usual to join together a number of rigid disks on a common axle to form a disk pack. Some rigid-disk packs have one surface set up as address fields (Fig. 3.5).

Rigid disks were introduced in the late 1950s, for mainframe computers. A modern development (circa 1976) of the early disks is the Winchester rigid disk in which the disk is fixed and cannot be removed. Both the disk and its read/write head are enclosed in a sealed container to avoid contamination from the environment, thereby improving performance by allowing finer tolerances.

Winchester disks require no routine maintenance and are very reliable, high-capacity disks.

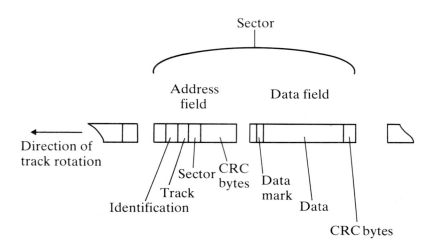

Fig. 3.4. A sector of a disk track.

Single disk surface

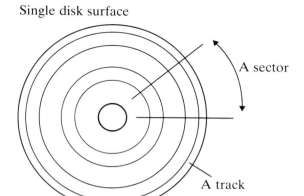

A sector

A track

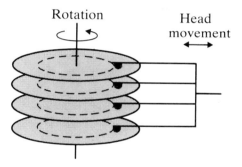

Rotation

Head movement

Fig. 3.5. Disk data layout and disk pack.

Rigid disks rotate at high speed and the read/write heads float above the disk surface on a cushion of air generated by the rotation speed. Typical head to surface separation is 20 micro-inches, much smaller than the diameter of a human hair. When rigid disks are stationary, the heads are retracted onto a landing pad, and only extended over the disk surfaces when these are rotating at full speed.

Floppy disks rotate at one-tenth the speeds of rigid disks and have the read/write heads in contact with the disk surfaces.

Table 3.10 gives a broad classification of disk formats.

Table 3.10. Popular disk formats.

Disk diameter (inches)	Rigid				Floppy
	Fixed		Exchangeable		
	Single	Pack	Single	Pack	
14	(W)	X	X	X	
8	W	W			(X)
5¼	W	W			X
3½	W	W			X
3 and smaller					X

key:
X = Disk products generally in use
W = Winchester type
( ) = introduction format (see below)

The advances in technology for rigid disks, Winchester disks and floppy disks have always been introduced with the larger diameter disks. As further advances are made, the larger diameter disks are less widely used and are often exceeded in storage capacity and other features by the smaller and newer disks of the same type.

An exchangeable disk pack is one which can be removed from the disk-drive unit for storage or use on other disk-drive units of a similar type. A disk cartridge is exchangeable, and part of the case remains with the drive to protect the disk when loaded onto the drive unit.

3.2.1 Rigid Disks

Non-exchangeable disk units are designed to maximize on-line storage capacity and/or data transfer rates. Multiple disk packs are used with one movable read/write head per surface, or multiple fixed read/write heads arranged as one per track. The latter feature reduces storage capacity but increases data transfer rates.

Many of the larger capacity disk units contain two or four disk packs each in a sealed unit with its own electronics and data paths. In fact, this type of unit is often called a Winchester type because of the sealed nature of the disk mechanisms.

Rotational speeds are typically 3600 rpm or 3000 rpm, but others such as 2160 rpm are also used. Average access time is the sum of the average read/write head movement time (with settling) and the latency. The data on a track move under a read/write head due to the rotation of the disk. It is unlikely that the correct portion of a track will be

Table 3.11. Characteristics of large non-exchangeable disk units.

Model	Disk drive capacity (Mbyte)	Number of drives per cabinet	Cabinet capacity (Gbyte)	Recording density (bpi)	Average access (ms)	Transfer rate (Mbytes/sec)	Features
IBM 3350	317.5	4	1.27	–	33	1.2	
Digital Equipment RA81	456	3	1.37	11400	36	2.2	Sealed head/disk assembly, dual read/write heads per disk surface.
Storage Tek 8380 (IBM 3380 standard)	630+630	2	2.52	–	24	3.0	Two access read/write assemblies per disk drive.
Control Data 9771	825	1	0.825	15400	30	1.8	Sealed head/disk assembly, rack mounting unit.
IBM 3380 double capacity	1260+1260	2	5.04	–	25	3.0	Two access read/write assemblies per disk drive.

positioned under the head when it is required. On average it will be one half revolution away from the head; this is taken as the latency.

Table 3.11 gives average access times for large-capacity disks.

For a speed of 3600 rpm:

$$\text{latency} = \frac{1}{2} \times \frac{60}{3600} = 8.3 \text{ ms}$$

Table 3.11 gives the characteristics of a selection of large non-exchangeable disk units. The term drive means a single multi-platter disk assembly, also called a spindle. The IBM 3380 units contain two drives, but each drive has two sets of independent read/write assemblies which access separate parts of the rotating media. In IBM notation this gives two volumes per drive, and thus four volumes per unit.

Large-capacity exchangeable disks are made of rigid alloy 14-inch diameter disks. Single disks are mounted in cartridge form; multi-platter packs are generally available with 5 or 12 disks. The top and bottom disks are not generally used for data storage on their outer surfaces, and may be present only as 'guard' disks. Some types of disk pack may have one surface pre-recorded for head positioning. This allows track and sector positions to be kept away from the data recording surfaces, and allows a high proportion of these surfaces to be used for data. Hard-sectored floppy disks have a similar feature.

Table 3.12 gives the characteristics of some exchangeable disk packs. The 'type' category indicates a typical application for this type of pack, which may be widely used by a range of manufacturers.

3.2.2 Winchester Disks

Winchester rigid disks contain sealed units which enclose the read/write head and disk to avoid contamination from the environment. The larger capacity units are discussed in Section 3.2.1; this section contains information on the smaller diameter disks with capacities of 500 Mbytes or less. The latest Winchester disk products are moving away from the 14-inch and 8-inch diameter disks to the 'second generation' 5¼-inch disks.

New Winchester products are available extending their versatility; for example, an exchangeable Winchester cartridge is now available. The heads and disk are present in each cartridge.

Table 3.13 indicates de facto standards for interfaces to Winchester disk units.

Table 3.12. Exchangeable disks.

Type	Recording density (bytes per inch)	Number of disks	Surfaces used for data	Unformatted capacity (Mbyte)
CDC 9766	6038	10	19	300
ICL EDS 200 and IBM 3300	4040	10	19	200
CDC 9750 and IBM 3300	4040	10	19	100
CDC 9762 and ICL EDS80	6038	3	5	80
IBM 2314	2200	11	20	30
DG 6070	4400	1	2	10
CDC 9427 and IBM 5440	2200	1	2	5

Table 3.13. Winchester disk standards.

Standard name	Application	Transfer rate (Mbits/sec)	New standard	Transfer rate (Mbits/sec)
Control data SMD	large disks	10	ESMD	15
Seagate ST506	5¼ and 3½	5	ESDI	10
Shugart SA100	5¼	—	—	—

Key:
ESMD = Enhanced SMD
ESDI = Enhanced Small Disk Interface

Table 3.14 indicates the broad characteristics for Winchester disk media.

Table 3.14. Winchester disk characteristics.

Disk size (inches)	Total unformatted capacity of unit (Mbytes)	Average access time (ms)	Transfer rate (Mbits/sec)
14	200–600	15–30	10–15
8	10–200	25–70	5–10
5¼	5–50	25–180	5–10
3½	5–10	50–100	5

Table 3.15 gives examples of 8-inch disk product specifications.

Table 3.15. Winchester 8-inch disks.

Model	Unformatted capacity of unit (Mbytes)	Number of disks	Recording density (bpi)	Average access time (ms)
Control data				
9715	165.9	6	10000	38
(9-inch)	344	7	9492	28
	516	7	15159	28
Mitsubishi				
M2860-3	85.37	4	10900	30
Shugart				
SA1106	33.9	3	6006	35
Quantum				
Q2020	21.33	2	6600	60
Fujitsu				
M2301BE	11.87	1	12360	70

Table 3.16 gives examples of 5¼-inch disk specifications.

Table 3.16. Winchester 5¼-inch disks.

Model	Total unformatted capacity of unit (Mbytes)	Number of disks	Recording density (bpi)	Average access time (ms)
Rodime				
R0208	53.3	4	10200	50
Quantum				
Q530	31.99	3	9200	45
Ampex				
Pyxis 13	13.33	2	8900	90
Seagate				
ST206	6.38	1	9074	85

For comparison, the recently introduced Rodime 3½-inch Winchester has the specification given in Table 3.17.

Table 3.17. Winchester 3½-inch disk.

Model	Total unformatted capacity of unit (Mbytes)	Number of disks	Recording density (bpi)	Average access time time (ms)
Rodime RO352	10	2	11000	85

3.2.3 Winchester Cartridges

Removable Winchester disks enclosed in cartridges are becoming available in the 5¼-inch size. The complete disk units are often reduced to the size of a comparable floppy disk unit.

In larger sizes (8-inch) removable Winchester cartridges act as a backup facility for units which also contain fixed Winchester disks. Cartridges are also available in 10½-inch and 14-inch diameters.

There is an ANSI standard under development for 8-inch and 5¼-inch disk cartridges to promote media interchangeability.

Table 3.18 gives examples of removable 5¼-inch disk cartridges.

Table 3.18. Winchester 5¼-inch cartridges.

Model	Unformatted capacity (Mbytes)	Average access time (ms)
DMA 5R	5	40
Seagate ST706	6.4	85
Western Dynex WD505	6.4	35

Table 3.19 gives examples of dual fixed and removable disk cartridges, part is removable and part is fixed in the unit.

Table 3.19. Dual disk cartridges.

Model	Disk diameter	Unformatted capacity (Mbytes) Fixed	Removable	Average access time (ms)
Atheneum Aegis 10/10	5¼	12.75	12.75	35
DMA 5/15	5¼	15	5	40
Control data	8	25	25	35

3.3 Floppy Disks

A floppy disk is a plastic (mylar) disk coated with magnetic material and enclosed in a square plastic envelope. It is not removed from the envelope and may rotate easily within it. The envelope has several openings to allow the read/write head, drive spindle and index sensor access to the disk (Fig. 3.6). It is available in 8-inch and 5¼-inch diameters.

Smaller size floppy disks, mainly 3½ inches diameter, are enclosed in a rigid plastic case with a shutter mechanism to protect the magnetic surfaces when not in use. An ANSI standard is being formulated for these 'microfloppys'. Disk products ranging from 4 inches to 3 inches in diameter are also on the market.

Data is recorded in FM (frequency modulation) format, or MFM (modified frequency modulation). Using FM both data bits and clock pulses are recorded on the disk, whereas using MFM the data bits only are recorded, which doubles the amount of data which can be stored using the same number of flux changes in the magnetic layer of the disk.

The FM format is also called single density, and MFM format is double density.

The number of tracks recorded on a disk may be 35, 40, 77 or 80. One or both surfaces of the disk may be used to store data.

The outermost track is numbered Ø and usually kept as a catalogue or directory of the contents of the disk.

Soft-sectored disks contain a small index hole, near the central spindle hole, to show the start of each track. Within a track individual sectors are identified by special bit patterns and address labels. Writing the sector details to a new disk is called formatting. These details use up some disk space and thus reduce the space available for storing data by between 12.5% and 20%.

Hard-sectored disks contain an index hole and a set of holes punched around the spindle hole. Each of these holes indicate a sector of a track. More of the disk is available for storing data than is the case in similar soft-sectored disks. However, different disk drive units are required for hard- and soft-sectored disks.

3.3.1 8-inch Floppy Disks

The standard format uses 77 tracks per side and a rotational speed of 360 revolutions per minute. Data may be recorded on one side or both sides in either single density or double density. (77 tracks per side is approximately a density of 48 tracks per inch. The higher track density of 96 tracks per inch, common for smaller disks, is not used because of media stability problems.)

Flexible plastic case

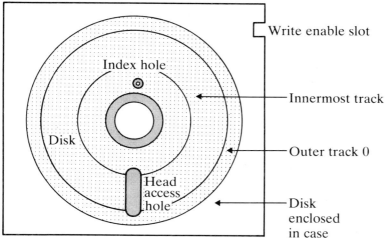

Fig. 3.6. A 5¼-inch floppy disk.

Table 3.20 summarizes the features of 8-inch floppy disks units.

Table 3.20. 8-inch floppy disks.

Side used for data	Unformatted capacity (Mbytes)		Average access time (ms)
	Single	Double	
1	0.4	0.8	90–270
2	0.8	1.6	75–100

Maximum data transfer rates are 32 Kbytes or 64 Kbytes per second.

Hard-sectored 8-inch floppy disks exist and usually have 32 sectors. Table 3.21 shows the formatted capacity for some of the popular soft-sectored formats and hard-sectored disks.

Table 3.21. Formats for 8-inch floppy disks.

Sides	Density	Sector	Number of sectors	Bytes per sector	Formatted capacity (Mbytes)
1	Single	Soft	26	128	0.250
1	Single	Hard	32	128	0.308
2	Double	Soft	8	1024	1.23
2	Double	Hard	32	256	1.23

3.3.2 5¼-inch Disks

The 40- and 80-track formats are widely used, although there are 35- and 77-track formats available. The rotational speed is 300 revolutions per minute. Data may be recorded on one side or both sides in single or double density. In addition, track spacing may be at 48 tracks per inch or 96 tracks per inch (giving the 40 or 80 tracks per side).

Single density (FM) recording implies a density of approximately 3000 bits per inch. Typical values are 2768 and 2938 bits per inch.

Double density (MFM) recording implies a density of approximately 6000 bits per inch. Typical values are 5876 and 5922 bits per inch.

Quad density, regarded as less reliable when first introduced is approximately 10 000 bits per inch. Typical values are 9868 and 11 844 bits per inch.

Table 3.22 summarizes the features of 5¼-inch floppy disk units. Values given for one side only; double the capacity values for double-sided disks.

Table 3.22. 5¼-inch disks.

Tracks	Density	Capacity (Mbytes)	
		Unformatted	Formatted
35	Single	0.1	0.078
40	Single	0.125	0.1
40	Double	0.25	0.2
77	Double	0.4	0.25
77	Quad	0.8	0.5
80	Single	0.25	0.2
80	Double	0.5	0.4
80	Quad	1.0	0.8

The maximum data transfer rates are 32 Kbytes or 64 Kbytes per second.

The 77-track 5¼-inch disk drive has characteristics similar to an 8-inch disk drive, for which it is sometimes used as a replacement.

Hard-sectored 5¼-inch disks are available with 10 or 16 sectors per track.

3.3.3 Sub 5¼-inch Disks

A 3½-inch diameter disk in a rigid plastic case seems to be emerging as a standard. This is an American microfloppy industry committee proposed standard, which is based on the Sony design (Fig. 3.7). It has several advantages over the larger floppy disks. A rigid case with shutter over the disk surfaces protects the disk effectively. The central spindle is a metal hub to ensure high positional accuracy.

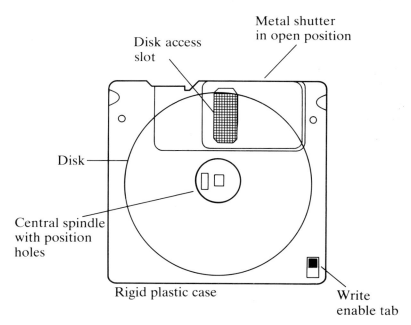

Fig. 3.7. A 3½-inch microfloppy disk.

There are some non-3½-inch products available in the small disk market.

Table 3.23 gives some examples of non-3½-inch disks.

Table 3.23. Sub 4-inch micro disks.

Manufacturer/ Model	Disk diameter (inches)	Sides	Unformatted capacity (Mbytes)
IBM	3.9	1	0.36
Tabar TC500/1000	3.25	1 or 2	0.5 or 1
BRG MCD-1	3	1	0.25
Hitachi HED 3055	3	2	0.25

Two groups of recording densities for 3½-inch disks are in use, one at approximately 4000 bits per inch and another at approximately 9000 bits per inch.

Track densities are at least 100 tracks per inch, with 135 tracks per inch as a possible standard. The latter gives 80 tracks on a 3½-inch disk.

Several manufacturers produce drives with a similar range of storage capacity which ranges from 0.25 Mbytes at single side and single density to 1 Mbyte at double sided and double density. Access times range from 100 ms to 500 ms depending upon the model. Drives in this group are:

Sony	OA-D32
Teac	FD35
Y-E Data	YD-600
MPI	351/352
Shugart	SA300 (one side only)

3.4 Mass Storage

Massive capacity storage devices based on electro-mechanical units which store hundreds or thousands of special tapes or tape cartridges are available. The tapes and tape cartridges are loaded automatically by the unit, which looks like a tape or disk system, to the computer. On-line storage ranges from 10 000 Mbytes to 1 000 000 Mbytes. Average access times are measured in seconds.

Optical disk units, based on laser technology using a write-once/ read-many-times system, are becoming available. The information recorded has an archive quality permanence, and average access times are only slightly longer than for magnetic disk units. Capacity per disk is greater than 100 Mbytes.

Table 3.24 gives specifications of mass storage devices.

Table 3.24. Magnetic media mass storage devices.

Model	Capacity (Mbytes)		Average access time (seconds)
	Minimum	Maximum	
IBM 3850	35 000	472 000	8–13
CDC 38500	16 000	1 000 000	7.5
Masstor M860	55 000	440 000	7.4

Optical disks, when writing, use a laser at high power to permanently alter a layer just below the surface of the disk (Fig. 3.8). The same laser is used at a lower power to read the marks, which are approximately one micron in diameter, from the disk. The write beam forms a bubble, hole or phase change in the material of the disk depending upon the technology of its construction.

Optical disks are removable from the drives. Although they are very tolerant to surface contamination, some models are enclosed in cartridges.

Table 3.25 gives examples of optical disks which are in production and available now.

Table 3.25. Optical storage media.

Model	Capacity (Mbytes)	Average access time (ms)	Sides used	Transfer rate (Mbytes/s)	Media
Storage Technology	4000	85	2	1.5	14-inch aluminium disk in cartridge
Hitachi	2600	250	2	0.13	12-inch in sealed cartridge
7640 Optimum 1000	1000	145	1	0.6	12-inch glass disk in cartridge
OSI Laser Drive 1200	1000	150	1	2	12-inch glass disk in plastic cartridge
Panasonic	700	500	–	0.6	8-inch plastic disk

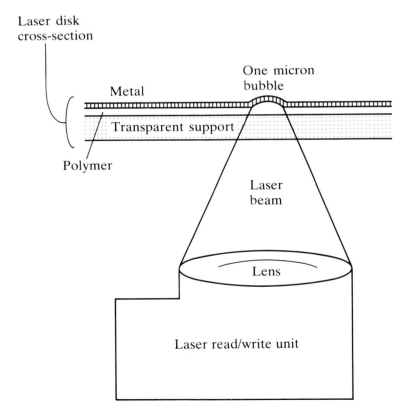

Fig. 3.8. Optical disk operation.

Chapter Four
Data Communication

4.1 Introduction

Data communication concerns the passage of information from a computer to another device. The method of moving data within a computer is not usually of interest to most computer users; however, many users are often concerned with the details of communicating with peripherals, such as terminals, printers and plotters, or indeed with other computers. This chapter describes some of the more common methods of achieving such communication, together with their associated standards.

4.1.1 Who's Who

Besides the computer manufacturers there are a number of bodies producing communication standards or providing communication services. Those most frequently encountered are briefly described below.

CCITT

The *Comité Consultatif Internationale de Télégraphique et Téléphonique* is that part of the United Nations agency *International Telecommunication Union* (ITU) concerned with telephone and data communication systems. Of the many recommendations produced by the CCITT are the 'V' series for data transmission over traditional telephone networks, and the 'X' series for dedicated data networks, some of which are summarized in Section 4.4.1.

ECMA

The *European Computer Manufacturers Association*. This is an association of data processing equipment manufacturers and other interested companies whose aim is to study and develop standards for the industry.

EIA

The *Electronic Industries Association* based in the United States of America. EIA-recommended standards are prefixed with 'RS', some of which are summarized in Section 4.4.2.

IEC

The *International Electrotechnical Commission.*

IEEE

The *Institute of Electrical and Electronic Engineers* based in the United States of America.

ISO

The *International Standards Organisation* which cooperates with the CCITT on telecommunication standards.

PTT

The *Post, Telegraph and Telephone* administration is a generic term identifying that body within a country which provides the telecommunication facilities. Some countries have more than one company providing this service, but, for convenience, the term 'PTT' is often used to cover them all.

4.1.2 Basic Concepts

Signals passing between a sender and a receiver may go through several different physical components, both transmission lines and other equipment. The term *channel* is therefore used to describe the logical path from a sender to a receiver. If the transmission is only ever in one direction this is known as a *simplex* channel. When communication is in both directions, but not simultaneously, it is possible for the same channel to be used, the direction of transmission being reversed each time; this is known as a *half-duplex* channel. A single channel cannot send information in both directions simultaneously, so that if this is required two separate simplex channels must be used; this is known as *full-duplex* working. Full-duplex channels do not, however, always require two distinct physical signal paths (Section 4.2.2).

Data communication is concerned with the transmission of binary digits, or *bits,* that make up the information being sent. Bits can either be sent one after the other, *serially*, or a number may be sent together, in *parallel.* Parallel transmission is normally only used for short distances (a few metres) because of the cost of the cable, all other transmissions being sent serially.

Most data communication standards do not refer to the connection of computers to terminals, being instead concerned with the connection of *data terminal equipment* (DTE), such as computers or terminals to *data circuit-terminating equipment* (DCE) such as modems (Section 4.2.2).

4.2   Peripheral Data Communication

This section is concerned with the transfer of data between a computer and a peripheral such as a terminal, printer or plotter. Communication with other computers is discussed in Section 4.3.

4.2.1 Serial Transmission

Serial transmission can be performed in a number of ways depending on the types of device that are communicating and the data to be transmitted. Two possible conditions must be transmitted — *mark* to represent a '1', and *space* to represent a '0'.

Asynchronous Transmission

Many devices such as terminals are character or byte oriented. In addition it is not possible to predict the number of bytes that are required to be transmitted at any time. Such random communication is known as *asynchronous* operation and each byte is dealt with individually.

When there is no byte being transmitted the channel is kept at the 'mark' condition. Immediately prior to sending a byte, a 'space' is transmitted to alert the receiver; this is known as the *start bit.* The byte of data is then sent, the least significant bit first. Finally, one or two extra bits are added. These are known as *stop bits* and their purpose is to ensure that the channel is at the 'mark' condition to enable the next start bit to be recognized. Mechanical receivers usually require two stop bits, whilst electronic receivers require only one. Figure 4.1 shows the transmission of the byte '01101010'.

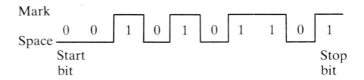

Fig. 4.1. Asynchronous transmission of '01101010'.

Synchronous Transmission

When a large number of characters are to be sent, the asynchronous system is rather inefficient since at least 20 per cent of the bits transmitted contain no data information. Another method of operation permits the synchronous transmission of characters. In this system a group of characters is sent as a single stream of bits, one character immediately following another. In between each group of characters a number of synchronization characters, such as ASCII SYN (00010110), are sent. The receiving equipment is capable of recognizing this character and synchronizing with it.

V24 and RS232C

The most common standard under which asynchronous and synchronous byte transmission is performed is the CCITT V24 standard, or the EIA RS232C standard, which for most practical purposes are identical. Two data values are used, $+V$ to represent a 'space' and $-V$ to represent a 'mark', where 3 volts $\leq |V| \leq$ 25 volts. The full standard is quite complex and so a number of different subsets are in common use. Although the CCITT does not define the physical plug to be used, most manufacturers use the ISO 2110 standard 25-way 'D-type' whose pin numbers will be used in the figures below.

BASIC DATA EXCHANGE

The simplest configuration is where a basic data exchange is required and only three lines are used, as shown in Fig. 4.2.

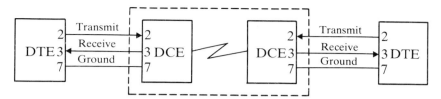

Fig. 4.2. Basic data exchange connections.

The DCEs are often omitted, the transmit line of one DTE being connected directly to the receive line of the other DTE, an operation sometimes performed by a *null modem* (see below).

CONTROL OF DIRECTION OF DATA

When working in half duplex it is necessary to be able to control the transmissions of a DTE. Three lines are used as shown in Fig. 4.3.

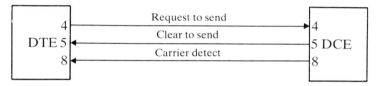

Fig. 4.3. Data direction control connections.

Request to Send (RTS) is set whenever the DTE wishes to transmit data, but it may not do so until the DCE has set *Clear to Send* (CTS). *Carrier Detect* (CD) is set whenever the DCE is receiving a carrier signal from another DCE on which data could be received. In half duplex, CD is unset whenever RTS is set.

DIAL UP TELEPHONE CONNECTION

When the DCE is a modem connected to a dial up telephone and is capable of receiving incoming calls, three additional lines are used as shown in Fig. 4.4.

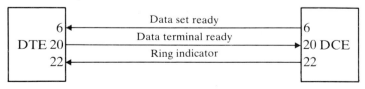

Fig. 4.4. Dial up telephone connection.

Data set ready (DSR) ('data set' is the American term for a modem) is set whenever the DCE is operational. *Data terminal ready* (DTR) is set whenever the DTE is operational, and is unset to terminate the connection. *Ring indicator* (RI) is set to coincide with the ringing tone of the telephone line.

SYNCHRONOUS TRANSMISSION

In order to achieve synchronous transmission a timing signal has to be sent so that the receiver knows when to sample each of the data bits. The clock providing this signal may be in the DTE or, more usually, in the DCE. A total of four possible lines are involved as shown in Fig. 4.5, although only three are used for any particular connection.

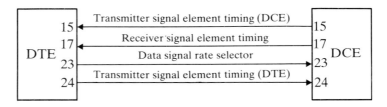

Fig. 4.5. Synchronous transmission connections.

Only one *transmitter signal element timing* signal is used. The line on pin 24 is chosen if the clock used to synchronize transmitted data emanates from the DTE, whilst the line on pin 15 is chosen if the transmitter clock signal is generated within the DCE. The *receiving signal element timing* signal is used for sampling received data. Some DCEs have a two-speed clock, the *data signal rate selector* being set to choose the higher speed, and unset for the lower speed to be used.

SECONDARY CHANNEL

Some DCEs have a low-speed secondary channel for auxiliary communication or supervision. A second set of lines is provided for this channel as shown in Fig. 4.6. Their function is similar to those of the primary channel above.

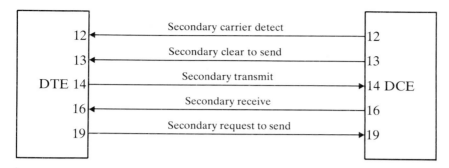

Fig. 4.6. Secondary channel connections.

WORKING WITHOUT DCES

When the distance between two devices is short it is often unnecessary to use DCEs explicitly. In this situation it is necessary to ensure that the two DTEs each receive the correct signals on the correct pins. This can be achieved either by crossing over the wires according to Fig. 4.7, or by using a device called a *null modem* which does the same thing.

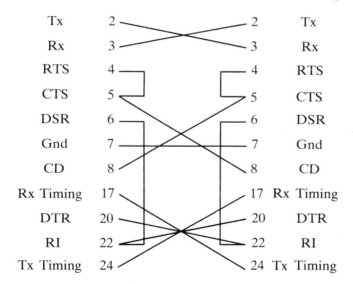

Fig. 4.7. Null modem connections.

On occasions some signals are used on their own; in particular, DTR usually indicates that a terminal is switched on, and CTS can be used to control the flow of data from a DTE in full duplex working.

RS422, RS423 and RS449

The electronic specifications of RS232C were developed before the widespread use of integrated circuits and the need for high data rates, but the standards RS422 and RS423 rectify this deficiency. In addition, the standard RS449 is beginning to replace RS232C for use with integrated circuits. Both RS423 and RS449 can, however, usually work with RS232C.

Current Loop

The original mechanical terminals operated using the presence or absence of a current to indicate a 'mark' or a 'space' respectively. The most popular system was the 20 mA current loop interface developed by TELETYPE. Some VDUs may also use this interface. Four lines are used, two for the receive circuit and two for the transmit circuit.

4.2.2 Modems

The simplest form of transmission is merely the sending of digital signals along the transmission medium. This is known as *baseband* transmission and is used for most unsophisticated short distance links.

For long distance communication this is not a suitable mechanism for electrical reasons. In addition, many countries grant the monopoly on all non-local communication to their respective PTT, and one therefore has to adhere to their regulations. The obvious system to use is the *Public Switched Telephone System* (PSTN). However, this equipment is designed for voice communication and is not suitable for digital transmissions.

The solution is to use a continuously varying (AC) signal onto which is superimposed the digital information. This is known as *modulation*. Consider a general sine wave

$$h(t) = \mathbf{a} \sin(\mathbf{f}t + \mathbf{p})$$

where $\mathbf{a}$ is the amplitude, $\mathbf{f}$ is the frequency and $\mathbf{p}$ is the phase. One, or more, of these three can be varied, or modulated, in time with the digital signal, and this variation can be detected at the receiver and *demodulated*. A device that will transmit and receive such signals is known as a *modem* (**mo**dulator–**dem**odulator). The effect of these three types of modulation is shown in Fig. 4.8.

Amplitude modulation (AM) is not normally used since it is susceptible to the attenuation in the PSTN which then confuses the signal. In *frequency modulation* (FM), sometimes called *frequency shift keying* (FSK), two or more tones are used to represent the digital values. In *phase modulation* the phase is shifted π/4, 3π/4, 5π/4 or 7π/4 thus giving four different data values, and therefore two bits of data can be sent at a time.

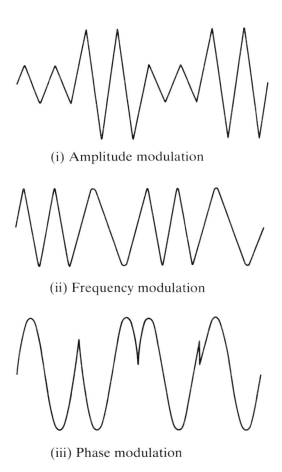

(i) Amplitude modulation

(ii) Frequency modulation

(iii) Phase modulation

Fig. 4.8. Modulation of waves.

In order to transmit information a range of frequencies is required around the fundamental frequency being modulated. This is known as the *bandwidth* of the channel and, in general, the higher the data rate the wider is the bandwidth required. The transmission medium itself also has a range of frequencies, or bandwidth, which it may transmit without too much distortion. The bandwidth of the transmission medium is usually much wider than the channel bandwidths, and so, by suitably choosing fundamental frequencies, more than one channel can exist within a single transmission medium. For example, full-duplex working requires two channels, and synchronous transmissions sometimes require additional channels for timing information, although in this case many DCEs reconstruct the clock from the data transmissions.

Public Switched Telephone Network

The PSTN has a very limited bandwidth. Frequency modulation is used to provide low speed (300 bits/sec) full-duplex operation. For complete mobility it is possible to use an *acoustic coupler* which takes the handset of any telephone (provided it is the correct shape!). Extraneous noise can, however, disrupt the communication, and in static situations it is therefore usual to have the modem wired into the PSTN.

Some applications require only very low speed operation in one direction, but high speed in the other. In this situation the high speed channel can use most of the available bandwidth, the low speed channel using part of what remains. This is sometimes called *split speed* working (e.g. 1200/75 bits/sec) and is used in viewdata applications.

Phase modulation permits higher data transmission rates (2400 bits/sec) within the PSTN bandwidth.

Leased Lines

To achieve higher speeds (> 2400 bits/sec) it is usually necessary to lease lines from the PTT, which bypass the exchanges where much of the useful bandwidth is lost. These are available at various prices according to the bandwidth required, and are point to point only.

Modem Protocols

The CCITT have defined a number of protocols for modems, summarized in Section 4.4.1, and it is therefore necessary to ensure compatibility between both ends of a modem communications link.

4.2.3 Multiplexors

Since the cost of installing cable is high, it is more efficient overall to force a number of channels to use a single cable. This is known as *multiplexing* of which there are three basic types.

Time Division Multiplexing

It would seem sensible to be able to put eight 300 bits/sec channels onto one 2400 bits/sec channel. This is indeed the case and in *time division multiplexing* (TDM) a time slot is allocated to each of the slow channels, which are polled in turn, and the data received is sent at the higher speed along the fast channel. The slow channels are then reconstituted by a *demultiplexor* at the other end.

Statistical Time Division Multiplexing

Simple TDM can be very inefficient since, although often there may not be any data to send for a particular slow channel, its time slot is still allocated on the fast channel. When using a *statistical time division multiplexor* (STDM), rather than being polled, the slow channels request that their data be sent. Obviously such a multiplexor, and its corresponding demultiplexor, must have sufficient intelligence to indicate who is sending what, but since it is very unlikely that all the slow channels will want to transmit at once, many more slow channels can be connected to a STDM than to a TDM.

Frequency Division Multiplexing

Frequency division multiplexors (FDM) take advantage of the wide bandwidth of most transmission media. They split the bandwidth into smaller subsets and each channel has added to it a frequency that will place it inside one of the subsets. Since radio frequency modems are required for this the system can be expensive.

Systems that use a single transmission medium for a number of channels are becoming known as *broadband* systems. Their importance is increasing, especially since any analogue transmission such as voice or television can be digitized and become one of the channels.

Multi-drop

Another method of sharing the same transmission medium between a number of terminals is by using a system known as *multi-drop*. All terminals share the same cable but, under the supervision of a *multi-drop controller*, only one terminal can receive or transmit at a time.

4.2.4 Binary Data Transmission

Byte oriented transmission, although perfectly suitable for transmitting characters, is not very suitable for transmitting binary data that has no such structure.

High Level Data Link Control

One common method of transmitting unstructured binary data is using the ISO *High Level Data Link Control* (HDLC) protocol. Three different types of communication are needed which are sent in *frames* as described in Fig. 4.9.

8	8	8	≥ 0	16	8
01111110	Address	Control	Data	Checksum	01111110

Fig. 4.9. HLDC frame.

The Flag Field
The bit pattern '01111110' is known as a *flag* and is used to delimit the frame. Since it is obviously essential that this pattern should not appear inside the frame a method known as *bit stuffing* is used. Whenever the transmitter encounters five consecutive '1s' inside a frame it automatically adds a '0' onto the bit stream; whilst whenever the receiver gets five consecutive '1s' followed by a '0' it deletes the '0'.

The Address Field
When used on multi-drop lines this identifies the receiver. For point to point lines it is sometimes used to distinguish commands from responses.

The Control Field
There are three types of communication which may be sent in a frame, and which are distinguished by the control field.

(1)   Information frame

This allows the data to be sent.

(2)   Supervision frame

Each information frame is acknowledged by the receiver so that if either an error is found, or the receiver does not respond at all (indicating that the frame has been lost), the sender can retransmit the information frame. This is known as *automatic repeat request* (ARQ). However, if there is a delay in obtaining the acknowledgement the system becomes inefficient. The solution is to allow a number of acknowledgements to be outstanding at any one time. Each information frame is given an identifying number from 0 to 7 as part of the control field. The receiver acknowledges these frames by returning the number of the next frame expected. Hence, up to seven unacknowledged frames may be outstanding at any instant. The frames being processed at any given point in time can be considered as a window onto the entire communication; consequently this is called a *sliding window* protocol.

(3)   Unnumbered frame

These are control frames used to send information such as 'Disconnect, I am about to go down (e.g. for maintenance)'. As these have no numbers associated with them only one control frame can be unacknowledged at any instant.

The Data Field

This is only present in an information frame.

The Checksum Field

Since the data field is of indeterminate length the checksum field is found by taking the sixteen bits prior to the terminating flag. The field is generated using a 16-bit cyclic redundancy code algorithm (Section 4.2.6).

4.2.5 Parallel Transmission

There are two common parallel transmission standards, both of which transfer an 8-bit byte of data at a time.

IEEE-488 Bus

The *IEEE-488 (1975)* bus, or Hewlett Packard *General Purpose Interface Bus* (HP-GPIB) from which it was derived, or *IEC 625 (1979)* bus is designed for interconnecting instruments. Its use with computers is still principally for interfacing with instruments, but a few microcomputers also use it for communicating with other peripherals, particularly disks.

There are three basic types of device, or any combination of them, on an IEEE-488 bus.

Talker
A device that can transmit data; only one device can talk at a time.

Listener
A device that can receive data; there is no restriction on the number of devices that can receive data at any time.

Controller
The device that controls the bus; only one at a time is allowed on any bus.

Signals on the bus conform to *negative logic* (low voltage = 'TRUE' or '1', high voltage = 'FALSE' or '0') so that any device signalling a 'TRUE' on a line overrides all other devices signalling 'FALSE'. Whilst data rates of up to 1 Mbits/sec are possible, the devices on the bus may all operate at different speeds. Up to 15 devices may be on the bus, but the maximum length of the interconnecting cable must be 20 m or twice the number (in metres) of connected devices, whichever is the less.

The IEEE-488 standard connector has 24 pins whilst IEC 625 uses the ISO 2110 25-pin 'D-type' connector. The designations are shown in Table 4.1.

The 16 active (i.e. not ground) signals are divided into three groups.

DATA BUS

The data bus consists of the 8 signals DIO1 to DIO8 along which bytes of data and other 8-bit parallel information (see below) are transferred.

TRANSFER CONTROL BUS

Three signals make up this group.

Data Valid (DAV)
Set 'TRUE' when a talker has put a byte on the data bus.

Not Ready for Data (NRFD)
Set 'FALSE' when a listener is ready to receive a byte on the data bus.

Not Data Accepted (NDAC)
Set 'FALSE' when a listener has received a byte from the data bus.

These three signals combine with the data bus to perform a three-way handshake whose timing diagram is shown, in Fig. 4.10.

Table 4.1. IEEE-488/IEC 625 bus connections.

IEEE Pin	Designation	IEC Pin
1	DIO1	1
2	DIO2	2
3	DIO3	3
4	DIO4	4
	REN	5
5	EOI	6
6	DAV	7
7	NRFD	8
8	NDAC	9
9	IFC	10
10	SRQ	11
11	ATN	12
12	SHIELD	13
13	DIO5	14
14	DIO6	15
15	DIO7	16
16	DIO8	17
17	REN	
	GND 5	18
18	GND 6	19
19	GND 7	20
20	GND 8	21
21	GND 9	22
22	GND 10	23
23	GND 11	24
24	LOGIC GND	
	GND 12	25

INTERFACE MANAGEMENT BUS

Five signals make up this group

End or Identity (EOI)
Set 'TRUE' by a talker to indicate the last byte of a message (not necessary).

Chapter 4

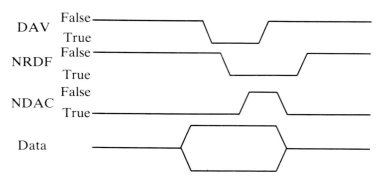

Fig. 4.10. IEEE-488 data transfer timing diagram.

Interface Clear (IFC)
Set 'TRUE' by the controller to reset all devices on the bus.

Service Request (SRQ)
An interrupt line set 'TRUE' by any device requiring a service from the controller.

Attention (ATN)
Set 'TRUE' by the controller to indicate that the byte on the data bus is control information (see below) rather than data. When used in conjunction with EOI it initiates a parallel poll sequence after an interrupt.

Remote Enable (REN)
Set 'TRUE' by the controller to inform any other device that could be a controller that it may not be one.

COMMAND BYTES

The command bytes that may be sent by the controller, accompanied by ATN, are summarized in Table 4.2. They are divided into five main sections. The *listen address group* (LAG) and *talk address group* (TAG) are used to specify the listeners and talkers respectively, with the *secondary command group* (SCG) providing further subdivision if necessary. *Address command group* (ACG) commands are sent to specific devices, whilst *universal command group* (UCG) commands are global.

Table 4.2. IEEE-488 command bytes.

Low order byte	High order byte							
	0	1	2	3	4	5	6	7
0			00	16	00	16	00	16
1	GTL	LLO	01	17	01	17	01	17
2			02	18	02	18	02	18
3			03	19	03	19	03	19
4	SDC	DCL	04	20	04	20	04	20
5	PPC	PPU	05	21	05	21	05	21
6			06	22	06	22	06	22
7			07	23	07	23	07	23
8	GET	SPE	08	24	08	24	08	24
9	TCT	SPD	09	25	09	25	09	25
A			10	26	10	26	10	26
B			11	27	11	27	11	27
C			12	28	12	28	12	28
D			13	29	13	29	13	29
E			14	30	14	30	14	30
F			15	UNL	15	UNT	15	31
	ACG	UCG	LAG		TAG		SCG	

Centronics Printer Interface

The Centronics Corporation has developed an 8-bit parallel interface for communicating with their printers which is also used by many other companies' printers. Such companies often modify the 'standard' slightly and so Table 4.3 shows only those signals and pin numbers corresponding to the main data and signal lines.

Data
The eight data lines provide the data for the printer; a high voltage corresponds to a '1', a low voltage to a '0'.

Data Strobe
Set low by the transmitter to indicate that valid data is on the lines.

Acknowledge
Set low by the printer to indicate that data has been accepted.

Busy
Set high by the printer whenever it is unable to accept data (e.g. because the buffer is full or the operator has switched the printer off-line).

Table 4.3. Centronics interface connections.

Pin	Data	Pin	Control
2	Data 1	1	Data Strobe
3	Data 2	10	Acknowledge
4	Data 3	11	Busy
5	Data 4	12	Paper End
6	Data 5	13	Select
7	Data 6	31	Input Prime
8	Data 7	32	Fault
9	Data 8	36	Input Busy

Paper End
Set high by the printer to indicate that it is out of paper.

Select
Set high by the printer to indicate that it is on-line.

Input Prime
Set low by the transmitter to reset the printer.

Fault
Set low by the printer when a fault has been detected.

Input Busy
Set high by the printer to indicate that data is being processed prior to 'Acknowledge' being given.

4.2.6 Error Detection and Correction

Transmitted data is always subject to possible corruption, either through external interference or noise within the channel. Various methods are available for detecting errors and some can also correct them.

Parity Checking

When transmitting 7-bit ASCII character codes an eighth bit is added, known as a *parity* bit, to bring the total number of '1s' in the resulting eight bits to an even number when working to *even parity,* or to an odd number when working to *odd parity.* Thus, assuming even parity, '1000011' becomes '11000011' and '1101010' becomes '01101010'. Even parity bits can be obtained by performing Exclusive-Or over all data bits.

Cyclic Redundancy Code

Parity checking will only find errors when an odd number of bits is wrong. The probability of detecting errors can be increased by using a method called the *polynomial code* or *cyclic redundancy code* (CRC).

Consider a series of bits as defining the coefficients of a polynomial, for example

$$11001 = 1x^4 + 1x^3 + 0x^2 + 0x^1 + 1x^0$$
$$= x^4 + x^3 + 1$$

Let the message be the polynomial $M(x)$, which is divided by a *generator polynomial* $G(x)$ of degree n. Thus

$$\frac{M(x).x^n}{G(x)} = M(x) + R(x)$$

where $R(x)$ is the remainder. Now form

$$P(x) = M(x).x^n - R(x)$$

which is the checksummed message to be sent and is n bits longer than $M(x)$. Since $P(x)$ is exactly divisible by $G(x)$ the receiver can check its validity by ensuring that it always has a zero remainder. Surprisingly the process of producing $P(x)$ and of checking it turns out to be quite simple when done in binary arithmetic, and hardware can be designed to perform it quickly. The polynomial of degree 16 used by V41 is

$$G(x) = x^{16} + x^{12} + x^5 + 1$$

Error Correcting Code

The above two methods merely detect errors, and correction must be performed by retransmission. Simplex channels, however, cannot request a retransmission and so *forward error correction* (FEC) has to be employed. A basic *Hamming code* that can do this is best described by a small example.

Bit number	111_2	110_2	101_2	100_2	011_2	010_2	001_2
Transmitted bits	d_3	d_2	d_1	c_2	d_0	c_1	c_0

Fig. 4.11. Hamming code example.

Consider the 4 bits of data $(d_{0..3})$ and the 3 check bits $(c_{0..2})$ shown in Fig. 4.11. Note that the check bits are placed in positions that correspond to a power of two (i.e. c_1 is at bit number 2^1); they are generated using the data bits with a '1' for that power of two in their bit number, thus

$$c_0 = d_0 \oplus d_1 \oplus d_3$$

$$c_1 = d_0 \oplus d_2 \oplus d_3$$

$$c_2 = d_1 \oplus d_2 \oplus d_3$$

Consider receiving the bit pattern '0100111' and calculate the check bits.

	Received	Error
$c_0 = 1 \oplus 0 \oplus 0 = 1$	1	No = 0
$c_1 = 1 \oplus 1 \oplus 0 = 0$	1	Yes = 1
$c_2 = 0 \oplus 1 \oplus 0 = 1$	0	Yes = 1

The error is therefore in bit $c_2 c_1 c_0 = 110_2$, and the bit pattern sent was '0000111'.

4.2.7 Data Encryption

Data transmitted over long distances is subject to possible interception, and it is therefore sensible to encrypt sensitive information.

Data Encryption Standard

In 1977 the US National Bureau of Standards adopted a cipher developed by IBM, which uses the same 56-bit key for both encryption and decryption. Known as *Data Encryption Standard* (DES) the algorithm has been implemented as an integrated circuit by a number of manufacturers, and is therefore fast in its operation.

In normal use the DES encrypts the data in blocks of 64 bits and is known as a *block cipher*. It is also possible, however, to arrange the circuitry so that it acts as a *stream cipher* which processes 8 bits at a time. This latter system is suitable for character transmission using V24 links.

Public Key Encryption

One of the problems with the DES is that the users at both ends of the communication need to know the key and to keep it secret. Consider a message M, an encryption algorithm E and a decryption algorithm D, then

$$D(E(M)) = M$$

It can be shown that it is possible to choose D and E such that E can be made public whilst D remains secret. By arranging that the algorithms depend on values of keys it is possible to make the algorithms public, one key public and the other key secret. Using such a system it is possible for anyone to send a secure message without having to be a party to a secret key.

4.3   Inter-Computer Communication

This section is concerned with the passage of information between computers. When communication lines are used for this data transfer the resulting system is called a *computer network*.

4.3.1 Topologies

To create a network of computers the *host* computers, which perform work for users, are each connected to a communications *node*. The resulting interconnection of these nodes produces the network. Figure 4.12 shows some topologies for connecting nodes together.

The *star* and the *loop* are examples of *point-to-point* networks where messages are sent from one node to the next and, if necessary, passed on. The *bus* and *satellite* are examples of *broadcast* networks where messages are sent to all nodes, but are only accepted by those for whom they were intended.

4.3.2 LANs and WANs

Networks can be divided into two broad categories. *Local area networks* (LAN) provide high speed communication between computers located reasonably close to each other, whilst *wide area networks* (WAN) provide a lower speed communication between computers located anywhere in the world.

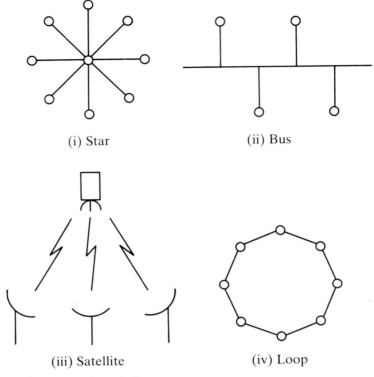

(i) Star   (ii) Bus

(iii) Satellite   (iv) Loop

Fig. 4.12. Some network topologies.

4.3.3 The OSI Model

When interconnecting computers it is necessary not only to define the physical link, but also to specify the types of messages that will be transferred. Most computer networks are designed in a structured manner. ISO has approved a structured model for interconnecting heterogeneous computer systems called *The reference model for Open Systems Interconnection* (OSI).

The model has seven layers as shown in Fig. 4.13. Each layer uses the facilities provided by its relative lower layer.

The Physical Layer

This is the layer at which the actual transmission takes place. The protocols are concerned with the transmission medium, the number of wires used, voltage levels and timing specifications, and other such electromechanical details (e.g. V24).

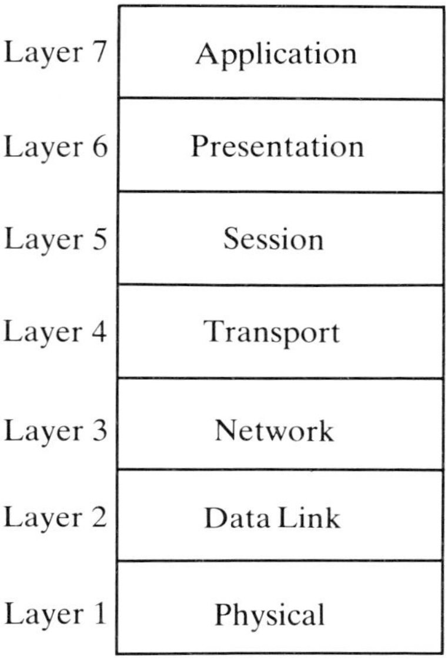

Layer 7	Application
Layer 6	Presentation
Layer 5	Session
Layer 4	Transport
Layer 3	Network
Layer 2	Data Link
Layer 1	Physical

Fig. 4.13. The OSI model.

The Data Link Layer

The purpose of this layer is to provide a reliable transmission path between two nodes (e.g. HDLC).

The Network Layer

The network layer is concerned with the routing of the communications from the source node to the destination node. This is particularly relevant in WANs where the communication may pass through a number of *switching nodes* en route from the source to the destination.

The Transport Layer

The transport layer is the lowest layer at which the host computers communicate directly with each other. The protocol provides the initial establishment of a communications channel, the transfer of data and the final release of the channel. For data transfer it interfaces with the network layer to provide an error-free virtual point-to-point connection, ensuring that the communications arrive in the right order and are passed to the correct process.

The Session Layer

The previous four layers have all been concerned with ensuring that a sequence of bits arrives uncorrupted at its destination. The session layer starts to add meaning to this data and provides some of the basic user orientated services, such as creating a process to perform a task and checking that the user has the privilege to do so.

The Presentation Layer

The presentation layer provides a number of specific and common services which can be called upon when required. Examples of these are *file transfer* and *virtual terminals*.

The Application Layer

This is the layer at which programs using the services provided by the network are written.

4.3.4 Network Standards

Standards are in the process of being produced for all seven layers of the OSI model. Those for layers 4 to 7 are still being worked on, but a number of standards already exist to provide the basic communication for both OSI and proprietary networks of homogeneous computers.

X25

The principal protocol used by PTTs to provide WAN communication facilities is the CCITT X25 standard. The physical layer for X25 is defined by X21; the data rates available depend on the PTT but can exceed 1 Mbits/sec. The data link layer is based on the ISO HDLC protocol (Section 4.2.4). The network layer splits messages into manageable sized chunks called *packets*. Each packet has its own 'header' that contains information describing the rest of the packet and indicating its destination. Packets are sent from node to node until that destination is reached, each packet being completely received by a node before being passed on (*store and forward*); the whole system being known as *packet switching*.

With X25, once a route has been found for the initial packet, a channel is set up along that route until the entire message has been passed, whereupon it is closed. This is known as a *virtual circuit.*

THE PACKET ASSEMBLER/DISASSEMBLER

To enable asynchronous terminals to use an X25 link a device is needed which will collect the characters from a number of terminals, create a proper X25 packet and send it to the host. Such a device is called a *packet assembler/disassembler* (PAD). Three CCITT standards define the use of PADs; X28 defines the terminal-PAD interface, X29 defines the PAD-DTE interface and X3 defines the parameters used by the PAD to control the terminal. A complete system is summarized in Fig. 4.14.

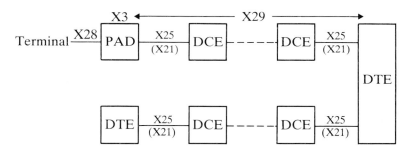

Fig. 4.14. CCITT PAD/DCE/DTE standards.

At first sight it looks as though X29 is a transport layer protocol. However, it requires certain features of, and is thus subject to, X25 from which a true transport layer would be independent.

Ethernet

Ethernet was originally designed by Xerox Corporation to provide the communication layers for their LAN. It has since become one of the OSI standards being defined by IEEE 802.3.

Ethernet is a high-speed (10 Mbits/sec) broadcast network using a single coaxial cable. Each node is tapped into the cable by drilling a hole in the insulation and fastening a transceiver to the central core. The resulting topology is shown in Fig. 4.12 (ii). It is a baseband network that uses a technique known as *carrier sense multiple access – collision detect* (CSMA–CD).

Before a node starts to transmit it listens to see if any other node is already using the cable (carrier sense) and if so waits until that one has finished. Once a node starts to transmit it is of course broadcasting to all the other nodes on the network (multiple access), each of which checks to see if it is the intended recipient of the message. Since it takes a finite time for signals to get from one end of the bus to the other there is a possibility that nodes at each end of the bus will both start to transmit simultaneously. Once their signals meet, garbage is produced and so an Ethernet transceiver listens to its own transmission; if it detects a difference it assumes that a collision of packets has occurred (collision detect) and stops the transmission. The other nodes that have been transmitting do likewise and the bus is cleared. To ensure that they do not all try again simultaneously each node waits a random time interval before trying again.

Messages are split into packets and sent in frames as specified in Fig. 4.15.

64	48	48	16	368–12000	32
Preamble	Destination	Source	Type	Data	CRC

Fig. 4.15. Ethernet frame.

Preamble Field
This is a standard bit pattern used to introduce the frame and allow the other transceivers to synchronize with the transmitter.

Destination and Source Addresses
The address of the destination and source nodes.

Type Field
This field is used by higher layers.

Data Field
The data field must be an integral number of 8-bit 'octets' but otherwise may be any stream of bits.

Cyclic Redundancy Check Field
A CRC using a generating polynomial of degree 32.

Ethernet is principally a passive system; there is no overall controller, each transmitter performing this task in turn.

Cambridge Ring

The Cambridge Ring was designed by workers at Cambridge University. A standard has been produced by the Joint Network Team of the Computer Board and Research Councils (JNT) called 'CR82' and it has recently been proposed that the Cambridge Ring should become one of the OSI standards.

The Cambridge Ring is a high speed ($\leqslant$ 10 Mbits/sec) baseband network using a protocol known as the *slotted ring*. The topology of a Cambridge Ring is that of Fig. 4.12(iv). A number of fixed sized mini-packets (or slots) circle the ring continuously, one bit of each mini-packet indicating whether the mini-packet is full or empty. Each node consists of a *repeater* which passes on each mini-packet to the next node whilst giving a copy to its attached *station*. When necessary, a repeater can substitute new data in the mini-packet. As the ring and nodes act as the store for all the mini-packets and most rings are not very large, in practice only two or three mini-packets circulate.

The format of a Cambridge Ring mini-packet is shown in Fig. 4.16.

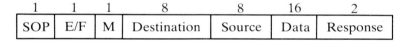

1	1	1	8	8	16	2
SOP	E/F	M	Destination	Source	Data	Response

Fig. 4.16. Cambridge Ring mini-packet.

Start of Packet (SOP) Field
A bit to indicate the start of the mini-packet.

Empty/Full (E/F) Field
If a station wishes to send information it has to wait for an empty mini-packet before it can do so. This is indicated by a '0' in the E/F bit. The station changes this to a '1' and then fills in the rest of the mini-packet. Whilst the destination node takes a copy of the mini-packet, it also passes it along the ring, filling in the response bits, so that it ends up back at the source. The source then checks that the data field has not been modified due to an error in the ring and changes the E/F bit to '0'. This way it is not possible for a node to monopolize the ring as it must await the next empty slot before continuing its transmission.

Monitor (M) Field
One station on the ring is a *monitor station*. It is not connected to a host and is responsible for maintaining the integrity of the ring and of the

mini-packets. The monitor field is used in conjunction with the E/F field. When a station fills a packet the E/F and monitor fields are set to '11', a station that empties a packet resets them to '00'. If a packet containing '11' passes the monitor station the bits are changed to '10', thus a packet containing '10' arriving at the monitor station must be in error.

Destination and Source Addresses
Each station on the ring is given an address and it is possible for a station to arrange to receive data from any source, a nominated source (used when receiving a large packet of data that is made up of many mini-packets) or indeed no source at all.

Data Field
Only 16 bits of data are sent with each mini-packet.

Response Field
These two bits are used to advise the source station what happened to its mini-packet. The possibilities are that:
(a)   The destination was switched off, or did not exist.
(b)   The destination chose not to receive from that source.
(c)   The mini-packet was accepted.
(d)   The station was too busy to receive it.

The Cambridge Ring is basically an active system; whilst it is possible for the stations to be switched off, the repeaters and the monitor station must be present at all times.

Token Passing

The principle behind *token passing* is that a single token is passed around all the nodes in turn, the token being necessary before transmission can be effected. This system can be applied to both rings and buses.

TOKEN RING

By removing the restriction that the packets must be stored entirely within the ring itself it is possible to allow transmissions of any length. This can be achieved by the transmitting node 'breaking' the ring and its receiver collecting the bits sent by its transmitter a short time previously. The token is passed on to the next node either after a single packet has been sent or after a specified time. A token ring standard is currently being defined by IEEE 802.5.

TOKEN BUS

The main difference between a token ring and a token bus is in the passing-on of the token. In a ring it is obvious that the next node in the ring will receive it, whilst in a bus a similar system would produce a problem when the end of the bus was reached. To solve this problem the network is set up so that each node sends the token to a specified successor. This way it is guaranteed that all the nodes will receive the token within a given length of time and the bus can in fact be considered as a 'logical ring'. A token bus standard is currently being defined by IEEE 802.4.

4.3.5 Applications of Computer Networks

Once computers have been connected together a variety of services become possible. These include:

File Transfer

This is used by many other services but the simple movement of data can be an end in itself.

Distributed Data Bases

In many large applications it is preferable to spread a data base across a number of computer systems.

Electronic Mail

A sender can create a document on his own computer and send it to the recipient's computer where it is stored until the receiver wishes to read it.

Value Added Network

Many WAN operators are beginning to provide services above simple message passing. These can include such facilities as electronic mail or the general exchange of orders and invoices.

Manufacturing Automation Protocol

The development of robots over the years has produced a variety of incompatible protocols used to control and monitor them. In order to alleviate this problem the General Motors Corporation has developed the *Manufacturing Automation Protocol* (MAP) to combine all aspects of production (e.g. programming robots, production monitoring, stock control, etc.). This standard is to be an implementation of the complete OSI model and uses broadband IEEE 802.4 token bus communications. MAP is now supported by many large industrial and computer manufacturers.

4.4   Summary of Selected Standards

4.4.1 CCITT

V10   Electrical characteristics for unbalanced double-current interchange circuits for general use with integrated circuit equipment in the field of data communications.

V11   Electrical characteristics for balanced double-current interchange circuits for general use with integrated circuit equipment in the field of data communications.

V21   200-baud modem standardized for use in the general switched telephone network.

V22   1200 bits/sec full-duplex 2-wire modem standardized for use in the general switched telephone network.

V22 bis   2400 bits/sec full-duplex 2-wire modem standardized for use in the general switched telephone network.

V23   600/1200-baud modem standardized for use in the general switched telephone network.

V24   List of definitions for interchange circuits between DTE and DCE.

V25   Automatic calling and/or answering equipment on the general switched telephone network, including disabling of echo-suppressors on manually established calls.

V26   2400 bits/sec modem standardized for use on 4-wire leased telephone-type circuits.

V26 bis   2400/1200-baud modem standardized for use in the general switched telephone network.

V27   4800 bits/sec modem with manual equalizer standardized for use on leased-type telephone circuits.

V27 bis   4800/2400 bits/sec modem with automatic equalizer standardized for use on leased telephone-type circuits.

V27 ter   4800/2400 bits/sec modem standardized for use in the general switched telephone network.

V28   Electrical characteristics for unbalanced double-current interchange circuits.

V29   9600 bits/sec modem standardized for use on leased telephone-type circuits.

V35   Data transmission at 48 Kbits/sec using 60–108 kHz group band circuits.

V36   Modems for synchronous data transmission using 60–108 kHz group band circuits.

V41   Code independent error control system.

X3   Packet assembly/disassembly facility (PAD) in a public data network.

X21   General purpose interface between DTE and DCE for synchronous operation on public data networks.

X21 bis   Use on public data networks of DTEs which are designed for interfacing to synchronous V-series modems.

X25   Interface between DTE and DCE for terminals operating in the packet mode on public data networks.

X28   DTE/DCE interface for a start/stop mode DTE accessing the PAD in a public data network situated in the same country.

X29   Procedures for the exchange of control information and user data between a packet mode DTE and a PAD.

4.4.2 EIA

RS232C   Interface between DTE and DCE employing serial binary interchange.

RS366   Interface between DTE and Automatic Calling Equipment for Data Communication.

RS422   Electrical characteristics of balanced voltage digital interface circuits (compatible with V11).

RS423   Electrical characteristics of unbalanced voltage digital interface circuits (compatible with V10).

RS449   General purpose 37-position and 9-position interface for DTE and DCE employing serial binary data interchange.

4.5 Bibliography

Cole R. (1985) *Computer Communications* (2nd edn). Macmillan Press, Basingstoke.

Deasington R.J. (1984) *A Practical Guide to Computer Communications and Networking* (2nd edn). Ellis Horwood Ltd, Chichester.

Fisher E. & Jensen C.W. (1982) *PET®/CBM and the IEEE 488 Bus (GPIB)* (2nd edn). Osborne/McGraw-Hill, Berkeley.

Jesty P.H. (1985) *Networking with Microcomputers*. Blackwell Scientific Publications, Oxford.

Scott P.R.D. (1979) *Introducing Data Communications Standards*. NCC Publications, Manchester.

Tanenbaum A.S. (1981) *Computer Networks*. Prentice-Hall, Englewood Cliffs.

Tugal D.A. & Tugal O. (1982) *Data Transmission*. McGraw-Hill, New York.

Chapter Five
Microcomputer Operating Systems

5.1 Introduction

Once the physical components of the microcomputer system have been assembled, some means of loading and executing programs must be provided. This is the province of the microcomputer's operating system.

When the microcomputer is powered on, it starts running a special program permanently stored in the memory. In very small microcomputers used mainly for games playing, a BASIC interpreter is also permanently stored in the memory, and is started automatically as soon as the startup program has initialized the hardware. This avoids having to read a large program from a slow, and unreliable, cassette tape recorder before the microcomputer can be used.

The larger microcomputer systems used for business purposes have much faster and more reliable disk drives as their primary storage medium. Most business applications require large working areas. It is, therefore, undesirable to have large areas of memory permanently filled with the operating system and the BASIC interpreter, which are only used occasionally. It is far better to keep most of these programs on disk and load them only when required. This makes the maximum possible memory space available to the current application program.

The startup program in a business microcomputer system is, therefore, very small. After it checks and initializes the hardware it then loads the central part of the operating system (or kernel) into memory, and passes control to it. The operating system will then load and execute the required applications program if it has been told to do so, or a special program which allows you to enter instructions to the operating system from the keyboard.

In addition to loading and executing programs, the operating system provides:

(a) a standard interface for programs to use basic input and output devices such as the keyboard, video display and printer,

(b) a standard method of reading and writing program and data files to disk,

(c) various utilities and housekeeping programs to maintain and update the files on disk. This includes the ability to list their names and other useful information as well as the ability to rename, copy or delete them,

(d) commands for swapping input and output between suitable devices. It is, therefore, possible to change the input from the keyboard to a disk file, or change output from the visual display unit to a printer or disk file.

In other words, the operating system can be considered to be a shell which cocoons the hardware and allows applications programs to be written for particular processors rather than individual computers (Fig. 5.1). The operating system deals with all the machine-specific operations. The applications programmer does not need to concern himself with whether a particular printer exists or is connected to the right input/output port; he just issues an instruction to print. The operating system does the rest.

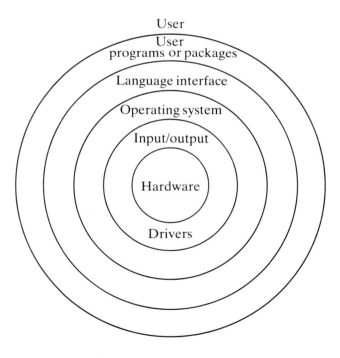

Fig. 5.1. The shell model of a computer system.

Traditionally, mainframe and mini-computer manufacturers have always developed their own system software. This has allowed them to take advantage of the special features that they had built into the hardware of their machines. This also had the advantage, for the manufacturer, that computer users were locked into that manufacturer, because the investment in programs and operating procedures was such that the cost of moving to a new machine range was totally uneconomic.

This situation lasted so long as the manufacturer was able to maintain a stable machine architecture. A range of models with different processing powers was available which allowed the user to upgrade to more powerful machines when the increased workload warranted it. The computer companies were able to absorb the high development cost of not only the operating system, but a whole range of other software, including compilers, linkers and applications utilities, in the high cost of the computing hardware. In fact, they usually provided all this software as part of the total computing package.

The coming of microelectronics and the resultant rapid fall in the cost of hardware have changed this. The mainframe and mini-computer manufacturers have often been left with outdated architectures from the 1960s or early 1970s, which they cannot afford to change because of the cost of redesigning the operating system and all the other systems software required to run a modern computer system. Although more computers are now sold they cost so much less, and profit margins are so much tighter that there are just not the revenues available for such a development. Users are now much more sophisticated. Applications programs written in standardized high-level languages can be moved to a microcomputer manufacturer offering all the facilities required, long before the original computer supplier can develop new facilities. The manufacturers had in fact locked themselves in as thoroughly as they had tried to lock in their customers.

The arrival of the microprocessor in the early 1970s highlighted these problems. It provided the means by which computers could be produced very cheaply with a standard processor architecture. The arrival of the floppy disk drive at about the same time provided the cheap, fast program storage medium needed for this type of system to take off. The problem was that each manufacturer wished to put these building blocks together in a different way. This, in effect, created a totally different computer system, such that programs written for one machine would not run on another. The much lower price of these machines and the decreased profit margins meant that only manufacturers who expected to sell many thousands of machines could afford the development costs of their own operating system. The answer was to develop a standard operating system for a particular processor that would allow software written for it to run on any computer built around that processor. The advantages of this approach were realized early in the development of microcomputer systems. To the computer manufacturer they include:

(a)   only having to provide input/output drivers which are cheaper and easier to develop than a complete new operating system,

(b)   the ability to use standard documentation provided by the software house, with the operating system, reduced development overheads and lead times,

(c)   access to a large body of development and applications packages which can be installed on the new machine with only a little customizing to work with the new keyboard and screen layouts.

The advantages to the microcomputer user include:

(a)   the availability of well-written manuals and books giving details of both the facilities provided and the use of the operating system,

(b)   access to a good range of software packages that can be purchased to run under a standard operating system. The larger user base means that the software is reliable with well-written documentation and books are available to describe how it can be used,

(c)   the ability to purchase microcomputers from different manufacturers without having to learn about several incompatible operating systems and applications packages. It should be noted, however, that new versions of both the operating system and those applications packages to be run on each machine have to be purchased. This is because the programs must be customized to the machines on which they run.

Three commonly used standard operating systems are now discussed in some detail. These are:

> CP/M (including CP/M-86 and CCP/M)
> MS-DOS (including PC-DOS)
> UNIX

The wide use of all these systems over a number of years has led to different variants being developed to take advantage of later changes in technology. In particular, they have been rewritten by the various software houses that originally wrote them to run on the newer families of microprocessors as they have become available. This has led to some considerable variation in the facilities offered by the different versions. This is particularly true when different generations of the same operating system are compared. These differences are usually enhancements rather than changes in what is already there. The facilities described in this chapter are therefore those which are common to all versions and should function in the manner described on all microcomputers equipped with the relevant operating system.

It is the intention of this chapter to introduce some of the basic functions common to all operating systems so that the facilities offered by each can be compared. These include:

> the user interface
> file management
> running programs
> facilities to tailor the system to your own needs
> input/output redirection

For a more detailed discussion of particular operating systems an extensive bibliography is provided in Section 5.6. It is also necessary to refer to the manufacturer's own manuals if the best use is to be made of an actual microcomputer. Minor differences do occur between different versions of the same operating system, and these should be explained there.

All three of these operating systems have a similar command interface by which a user initiates the required operation by typing in a command line consisting of a program or command name followed by a series of parameters. This is fine for experienced users who can remember both the command name and the order and form of the parameters. Casual and inexperienced users find this very off-putting. There have therefore been many attempts to define a better user interface. This has culminated in the development of Window, Icon, Mouse, Pull-down screens (WIMPS) Systems in which commands are replaced by small pictures which are pointed to with a small tracking device called a mouse. Options can be selected by pulling down menus from the top of the screen. This provides a simple command interface which does not require the user to remember large amounts of detailed information which is not relevant to the job in hand. All the options are displayed on the screen when they are required.

Some manufacturers have developed machines with completely new operating systems (such as the Apple Macintosh) to take advantage of the new facilities. This has the disadvantage that a whole set of new application packages has to be developed, and this takes time. The investment in the 'industry standard' operating systems is so large that their originators have attempted to gain as many of the advantages as possible whilst retaining the ability to run the popular packages. So:

(a)   IBM have developed Topview to run over MS-DOS,

(b)   Digital Research have developed GEM to run over CP/M-86 and CP/M-68K,

(c)   Microsoft have developed MS-WINDOWS to run over MS-DOS.

It is likely that large numbers of the microcomputers purchased in the future will have the ability to run one of these user interfaces, even if it is not included as part of the machine package.

5.2   CP/M

CP/M was one of the earliest attempts to develop a general operating system. It was developed by Gary Kildall while he was working as a consultant for Intel. He was working on the first PL/M (Programming Language for Microcomputers) compiler. Kildall designed CP/M to support a resident PL/M compiler. Although PL/M was adopted as Intel's main systems implementation language for the 8080 series microprocessors, in place of the assembly languages that they had used before, they were happy to continue using their mainframe cross-compilers for several more years. Kildall, therefore, broke with Intel and marketed CP/M himself.

The first major commercial customer was IMSAI, a very early pioneer in the development of microcomputer systems. By this time an assembler, debugger and an editor had been added to make CP/M a complete development system. A BASIC interpreter and various compilers soon followed. CP/M was soon well established as the standard operating system for 8080 and Z80 based microcomputer systems.

Since the early days CP/M has developed a long way. Digital Research have rewritten the operating system for the more recent Intel 8086 family microprocessor family, making it one of the few operating systems to survive a change in processor architecture.

There are now several versions of CP/M.

(a)   CP/M-80 — the original CP/M which runs on the 8080, 8085 and Z80 eight-bit microprocessors.

(b)   CP/M-86 — rewritten to run on the 8086 family of microprocessors.

(c)   CCP/M (or concurrent CP/M) — the multi-user variant which runs on the 8086 family of microprocessor.

(d) Concurrent PC-DOS runs on the 8086, 8088, 80186 and 80286 microprocessors and allows the running of standard PC-DOS/MS-DOS applications (see Section 5.3).

(e) Concurrent 286 is a multi-user, protected mode version for the 80286 microprocessor.

(f) CP/M-68K is a version of CP/M which runs on the Motorola 68000 series of processors.

It should be noted that although many applications packages are available under two or more different versions of CP/M, only that suitable for the particular processor family (8080, 8086 or 68000) used can be run on any individual microcomputer. It is, therefore, necessary to purchase a new copy of the software when upgrading the micro-computer system. However, once this has been done, it is possible to transfer files directly to the new microcomputer so that they can then be used with little or no modification on the new system. There is usually no problem in transferring BASIC programs, but for those written in other languages that are compiled into the microprocessor's own object code, the source text must be transferred and it is then recompiled to produce the new object module.

5.2.1   The Structure of CP/M

When writing programs, it is usually necessary not only to know on which microprocessor they will run, but also the memory organization and the input/output available. Both of these are the province of the microcomputer designer and can differ considerably between machines. CP/M aims to provide a universal environment in which programs can be written without any knowledge of the peculiarities of any individual system.

CP/M, therefore, defines its own memory map to which any micro-computer manufacturer wishing to run it must conform. Figure 5.2 shows how the memory is partitioned in CP/M-80. The other versions of CP/M follow a similar arrangement. The advantage of putting the main part of CP/M at the top of memory is that the writers of CP/M do not need to know where the different operating system routines are located. All communication with them passes through the reserved area in low memory. This allows a program that runs on one machine to be transfer-red without difficulty to any other machine running the same version of CP/M so long as there is sufficient free memory.

It is much more difficult to handle the wide variety of input and output devices available. Special driver routines must be written with a standardized interface to both user programs and other parts of the operating system.

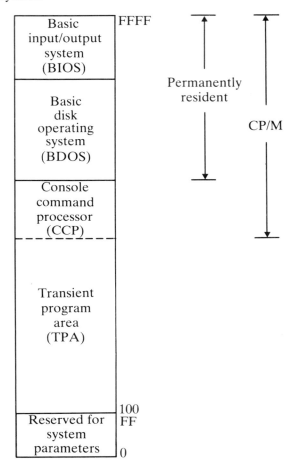

Fig. 5.2. CP/M-80 storage allocation (CP/M-86 is similar).

CP/M is divided into four logical components.

1   The Console Command Processor (CCP) handles the input and interpretation of commands from the keyboard.

2   The Basic Input/Output System (BIOS) looks after the transfer of data to and from the peripherals connected to the microcomputer system. It must be rewritten for each microcomputer system.

3 The Basic Disk Operating System (BDOS) looks after the management of files and other high-level functions such as reading and writing strings. The actual hardware-dependent functions are handled by the BIOS through standard interfaces so that no changes are required to the BDOS when CP/M is mounted on different microcomputer systems.

4 The Transient Program Area (TPA) is the area of memory into which user programs are loaded.

This means that it is only necessary to rewrite the BIOS to mount CP/M on a new microcomputer system since all system-dependent operations are performed through it. Once this has been done, applications programs can be transferred directly.

Input and output to standard devices must be dealt with in a standard manner so that the advantages of this flexibility are maintained. This is done by allowing user programs (and CP/M) to communicate with all the usual system peripherals by means of logical devices with a standard set of characteristics which are then mapped onto a set of physical device drivers located in the BIOS within CP/M. This allows the user to change the current device very easily to meet the needs of his installation or even a particular application. For example, it is quite common for a microcomputer system to be connected to two different printers, a fast dot-matrix one for proof copy and a slower daisywheel printer for final letter-quality output. With CP/M it is a simple matter to connect both printers to appropriate ports of the microcomputer and CP/M is then told which printer it is to use for any particular application. In practice, it is often easier to set up two copies of CP/M on different disks and swap disks, rather than remembering to reconfigure CP/M each time.

CP/M supports four logical devices, namely CON:, RDR:, PUN: and LST: (the colons are part of the names).

1 CON: designates a low-speed device for communications between the user and CP/M. It has three logical device drivers associated with it:

(a) CONIN inputs one character at a time from the console input device;

(b) CONOUT outputs one character at a time to the console output device;

(c) CONST examines the console input device to determine its 'character ready' or 'character not ready' status.

2 RDR: designates the logical reader device used for input from mass storage devices. Its logical driver is called READER.

3   PUN: designates the logical punch device used for output to mass
storage devices. Its logical driver is called PUNCH.

4   LST: designates the logical listing device. It normally directs the
output of a program to the printer, but in some cases sends the output to
a mass storage device other than disk. Its logical driver is called LIST.

Before any of these logical devices can be used they must be mapped
onto one of the physical devices (see Table 5.1). Sensible defaults are
usually defined when CP/M is installed on a new microcomputer. These
can, however, be changed to meet the needs of an individual user. The
method by which this can be done differs quite considerably between
different microcomputers and the relevant systems documentation
should always be consulted.

Table 5.1. CP/M-80 — some typical physical devices.

TTY:	Teletype device
CRT:	CRT device
BAT:	Batch mode (RDR input and LST output)
PTR:	High-speed reader device
PTP:	High-speed punch device
LPT:	Line printer device

5.2.2 Using CP/M

One of the major features of the CP/M family of microcomputers
operating systems is that, although there are detailed differences in the
way that each version operates internally, the interface that the user
sees is essentially the same. This allows the user to transfer to a new
microcomputer without the trauma of learning a new operating system.

When CP/M boots up it defaults to the disk in drive A and prompts
for input. Disk drive letters are defined by the microcomputer's manufacturer. The user is invited to type a command by the prompt:

A>

at the start of the next line. While CP/M is waiting for input certain
control characters have a special effect and these are summarized in
Table 5.2. The most important is <CTRL-C> which, when typed as the
first character after the prompt, performs a warm boot of CP/M, that is

the CCP and BDOS parts of CP/M are re-read into memory from the disk. This is done so that applications programs running in the Transient Programming Area can use the space occupied by the CCP and BDOS. Most applications, however, do not use the memory occupied by the BDOS. It is also necessary to type a <CTRL-C> before accessing a disk drive after the disk has been changed otherwise the disk becomes read-only. The <CTRL-C> causes the computer to read the disk directory (catalogue).

Table 5.2. CP/M control character functions.

Control character	Meaning
CTRL-C	reboots system from drive A (sometimes called a warm start)
CTRL-E	moves the cursor to the beginning of the following line without erasing the previous input.
CTRL-H	moves the character left one character position and deletes the character
CTRL-I	moves the cursor the next tab stop, where tab stops are automatically placed at each eighth column
CTRL-J	moves the cursor to the left of the current line and sends the command line to CP/M
CTRL-P	outputs everything sent to the console display until another CTRL-P is pressed
CTRL-M	moves the cursor to the left of the current line and sends the command line to CP/M
CTRL-R	types a // at the current cursor location, moves the cursor to the next line and retypes any partial command so far typed
CTRL-S	stops output to the console until another key is pressed
CTRL-U	discards all the characters in the command line so far typed, types a // at the current cursor position and moves the cursor to the next command line
CTRL-X	discards all characters in the command line typed so far, and moves the cursor back to the beginning of the current line
CTRL-Z	end of file

The code that makes up the resident parts of CP/M is stored on specially reserved tracks of the boot diskette and therefore does not appear in the disk directory. It must, however, be copied into the reserved tracks after the diskette has been formatted before the system can be booted from that diskette. This is often done by running a special program supplied by the machine vendor as part of the operating system package.

Built-in Commands

There are two types of command in CP/M, built-in and transient (see next section). The CCP will take the input and test to see if it is a built-in command and, if so, execute it. If it is not, it will access the disk to see if it is a transient command and carry it out if it is. If it is neither, it redisplays the input followed by a question mark and re-prompts for input.

If ':' is the first character on a line, CCP will ignore that line. This is not of use when typing from the keyboard but is of great help when a file of commands is created and later run using SUBMIT, for example

:THIS IS A COMMENT LINE IGNORED BY THE CCP.

'd:' selects drive 'd' as the default drive. All subsequent commands that do not specify a drive will use drive 'd'. CP/M allows up to 16 drives. For example, 'b:' will change the default to B and the CCP prompt will become

B>

All the remaining built-in commands require a file reference, which in CP/M consists of a file name and a file extension separated by a dot. If the file is not stored on the current default disk, the filename must be

Table 5.3. Some CP/M file types.

File types	Description
.COM	Command file (CP/M-80)
.CMD	Command file (CP/M-86)
.LST .PRN	Printable output
.$$$	Temporary file
.ASM	8080 Assembler source file (CP/M-80)
.A86	ASM-86 Source program (CP/M-86)
.H86	Assembled ASM-86 Program in hexadecimal format (CP/M-86)
.HEX	Code file in Intel hexformat (CP/M-86)
.SUB	List of commands to be executed by SUBMIT
.BAK	Backup file (normally a copy of the file before the last edit)
.BAS	BASIC Program
.COB	Cobol source program

preceded by the drive letter, followed by a colon. So a CP/M filename has the form:

<drive letter>:<filename>.<extension>

The extension indicates the type of information that is stored in the file to CP/M. Some of the most likely extensions are given in Table 5.3.

In addition to being able to give a complete filename, which refers to a single file such as:

statistics.dat

it is possible to refer to groups of files on the same disk. This is done by using special characters called 'wild cards'. CP/M recognizes two wild cards.

*   which matches any string, and

?   which matches any single character.

So that, for example:

*.dat

will match any file on the default disk whose suffix is '.dat', and

month?.dat

will match all of:

month1.dat
month2.dat
month3.dat

If the complete filename is used, it is called an unambiguous file-name (<ufn>), whereas if wild card characters are included it is called an ambiguous filename (<afn>). Wild cards cannot be used for the drive specifications.

File Management

ERA <afn> or ERA <ufn> will erase files specified from the directory of the drive named. If no drive is specified, the currently selected default drive is used. If '*.*' is typed as the <afn>, the CCP will prompt

'ALLFILES (Y/N)?'

and will only delete the files if 'Y' is typed in response, e.g. 'ERA
*.LST' will erase all files with the extension '.LST'. This might be used
to remove all the listing files from a diskette after they have been
printed.

DIR<afn> or <ufn> will display a list of the files that occur on the
specified drive. The command DIR without an <afn> or <ufn> can be
used to get a display of all files on the currently selected default drive.
For example

DIR B:*.LST

will display a list of file references for all files with the extension 'LST'
on drive 'B'.

REN <ufn1> = <ufn2> will rename the file <ufn2> as <ufn1>.
Both <ufn1> and <ufn2> must be on the same drive. If a drive name is
specified then it must be the same for both drives. For example

REN B:CHAPTER.OLD=B:CHAPTER.TXT

will rename the file 'CHAPTER.TXT' on drive 'B' as 'CHAP-
TER.OLD'.

SAVE <n>   <ufn> will save <n> pages of 256 bytes starting at
location 100H to the file specified by <ufn>. For example

SAVE 4 BUFFER.DAT

will save 1K of memory starting at location 100H to the file BUFFER-
.DAT on the currently selected default drive.

TYPE <ufn> will display the contents of the file specified on the
screen. For example

TYPE B:MEMO.TXT

will display the contents of the file 'MEMO.TXT' on drive 'B'.

Transient Commands

All other commands are known as 'transient commands' and require a
file with the name:

<command>.COM

in CP/M-80 or

<command>.CMD

in CP/M-86 to be present on the current default disk. This is a particularly convenient method of operation, as additional commands can be made available by simply transferring the appropriate files. The system is therefore inherently very adaptable and different suppliers will provide packages that are most suitable for the system on which it is intended to run. The commands described here are therefore only a selection of those that might be found on a typical system.

Some of the more commonly used transient commands include:

STAT   which allows the user to display the status of various operating system functions,

SUBMIT   which interprets command files and

PIP   which copies files from one part of the system to another.

Displaying Status Information

STAT allows the user to perform a series of system display functions. It also allows the user to set and clear the 'system' and 'read/write' flags from file entries in the disk directory.

CP/M will not allow you to write to a file or erase it when the 'read/write' flag is set to 'read/only'. This provides useful protection for essential programs and data files.

For example, the file 'CUSTOMER.DAT' can be protected by typing the command:

STAT CUSTOMER.DAT $R/O

and can be modified or erased after executing:

STAT CUSTOMER.DAT $R/W

If

STAT

is typed on its own, it will display the amount of space available on each active storage device, together with whether or not it is write protected. For a two-drive system with the B disk write-protected, the resulting display would look something like:

A: R/W, SPACE:nnnnK
B: R/O, SPACE:nnnnK

If a drive letter is provided as a parameter then the amount of space remaining on only that disk is reported.

It is also possible to display all the possible logical and physical assignments using the command:

STAT VAL:

and those that are actually set with:

STAT DEV:

Obtaining and Modifying Directory Information

It is possible to tell CP/M that a file has 'system' status and should therefore not appear in directories produced using the 'DIR' command. This is particularly useful for hiding files required for CP/M transient commands, such as 'STAT.COM', the STAT command file.

This can be hidden by typing:

STAT STAT.COM $SYS

and will appear in a 'DIR' listing again after typing:

STAT STAT.COM $DIR

The general form for this type of usage is thus:

STAT <afn> $<option>

where <option> is one of 'R/O', 'R/W', 'SYS' or 'DIR'

It is also possible to tell CP/M not to write to a particular diskette. This is done with a statement of the form:

STAT <drive>=R/O)

For example, drive B can be protected by typing:

STAT B:=R/O

This protection can later be removed by typing:

STAT B:=R/W

Batch Processing

It is often necessary to repeat a whole series of commands every time that you wish to perform some specific tasks. This is both time consuming and error-prone. CP/M therefore provides the facility to create a file containing all the necessary commands with the name

<filename>.SUB

all of which are executed when the command

SUBMIT <filename>

is typed. In Concurrent versions this command is called BATCH. To provide greater flexibility it is possible to use parameters inside the command file, these being symbolically represented by $1, $2, $3, etc. These parameters are specified as a list following the filename when calling the command procedure:

SUBMIT <filename> <parameter1> <parameter2>....

It is thus possible to write a command procedure 'LIST.SUB' which will display a file with a suffix '.LST' to the console and then delete it. For this example, all files are assumed to be on the same disk. The file 'LIST.SUB' would need to contain:

TYPE &1.LST
ERA $1.LST

and it would be called by:

SUBMIT LIST <filename>

Copying and Listing Files

No means of copying files or listing them to a printer or other peripheral have so far been described. All these functions are performed using PIP (Peripheral Interchange Program). Not only will PIP copy files, but it will also copy whole volumes, or transfer files to or from peripheral devices.

PIP can be used either in interactive mode where only:

PIP

is typed. PIP then responds with its own special prompt:

        *

It is then possible to type commands to PIP which are then executed. To return to CCP the 'return key' is pressed without typing anything else on the line.

If only one PIP command is to be issued it can be added as a parameter to PIP, saving some time. PIP command lines always have the same form:

        <destination> = <source>

so

        TEMP.TXT = PAPER.BAK

copies the content of 'PAPER.BAK' into 'TEMP.TXT' on the currently logged drive and

        B:=*.TXT

copies all the files with the extension 'TXT' from the currently logged drive onto drive 'B'. This is a very useful facility for backing up only the useful information on diskettes.

It is possible to concatenate files by listing them in the source field, so:

        BOOK.LST = C1.LST, C2.LST, C3.LST, C4.LST, C5.LST

would make up a file 'BOOK.LST' which contains the contents of 'C1.LST', 'C2.LST' and so on, in that order. This allows sections of a large document, such as a book, to be prepared in manageable chunks and then combined for final printing.

PIP can also be used to list files by using a Logical Device Name, rather than a filename for one of the codes. So:

        CON:=PROG.LST

will list 'PROG.LST' to the console screen, whereas

        LST:=PROG.LST

will send it to the system printer.

        TEST.DAT=CON:

will take input from the console keyboard and enter it into the file 'TEST.DAT'. Input is terminated by the end-of-file character (CTRL-Z).

Running Your Own Programs

There is, in addition, the possibility of the user adding his own programs. These can be called in the same way as transient commands, and so long as the user follows the standard CP/M conventions he can also read additional parameters on the command line. If the command name is prefixed by a drive letter:

<drive> : <command>

CP/M will look for the appropriate file on that drive. To this end CP/M-80 is normally supplied with:
(a) a simple line editor (ED),
(b) an 8080 assembler (ASM), and
(c) an extensive 8080 machine code debugger (DDT).

With CP/M-86, similar facilities must normally be purchased as optional extras.

In addition, it is possible to purchase compilers for a whole range of different languages such as COBOL, Fortran and Pascal which will generate the appropriate command files as their final output.

Finally there must be programs to:
(a) format disks,
(b) maintain the systems tracks and copy CP/M to make a bootable disk,
(c) copy complete diskettes including systems tracks.

These are often provided by the microcomputer manufacturer, and so are not standard across all implementations of CP/M. The programs are therefore usually described in machine-specific supplements to the standard CP/M documentation.

5.3 MS-DOS

In 1981 Microsoft were already well known to microcomputer users as the supplier of BASIC interpreters to almost all of the first generation of microcomputer systems. Their particular dialect for what was until that time the most non-standard of computing languages became the new standard. It was, therefore, something of a surprise to many people that IBM went to Microsoft for the principal operating system for their new sixteen-bit computer rather than CP/M-86.

MS-DOS, therefore, came into the new sixteen-bit microcomputer market with a flying start. Microsoft immediately supplied their industry-standard BASIC interpreter as part of the package (unlike CP/M where it had until then usually been an extra). The marketing power of IBM meant that all the best selling packages running under CP/M were soon rewritten to run under MS-DOS. The increased speed and memory capacity available with the new machine have allowed:
(a)   more facilities to be added,
(b)   more data to be handled,
(c)   and a much improved user interface to be provided.

As more manufacturers have entered the sixteen-bit market they have included MS-DOS as part of the package, so that the packages already available for the IBM personal computer could be transferred to their microcomputer with the minimum of delay.

IBM market MS-DOS as PC-DOS since there are detailed differences from the generic MS-DOS to take account of the IBM personal computer's particular architecture.

5.3.1 The Structure of MS-DOS

Whilst many MS-DOS commands bear a striking resemblance to the equivalent CP/M command the internal structure of the operating system is very different. In fact it more closely resembles Unix (see Section 5.4), or rather Microsoft's own microprocessor version of that operating system (called Xenix). This is particularly true of the file handling facilities where:
(a)   the directory structure,
(b)   input and output redirection, and
(c)   pipes
are all features that were pioneered in Unix.

While MS-DOS retains the CP/M idea of drive names, the larger disk sizes, particularly of fixed Winchester disks, have made it necessary to be able to maintain a number of different directories (each contains a list of filenames) on a single volume if directory sizes are not to get totally out of hand. It is, for instance, possible to hide most of the MS-DOS system files by placing them in their own separate directory.

Figure 5.3 shows a typical organization of MS-DOS directories. Each disk has its own directory structure. This means that the full filename must specify the disk on which it resides. The main directory on each disk is called the 'root' directory (written as '\'). Subdirectories are identified by name followed by another '\'. The filename is then given followed by a period and the file extension. The file extension must be present, and a list of those commonly used is given in Table 5.4. The full filename therefore has the form:

<drive> | <directory list>\<filename>.<extension>

where the <directory list> has the form:

<directory>\ ..... \<directory>

The files shown in Fig. 5.3 would therefore have the following file-names, assuming that the disk was in drive c:

c:\Accounts_Data\Last_month\Cashbook
c:\Accounts_Data\Last_month\Ledger
c:\Accounts_Data\Last_month\Payroll

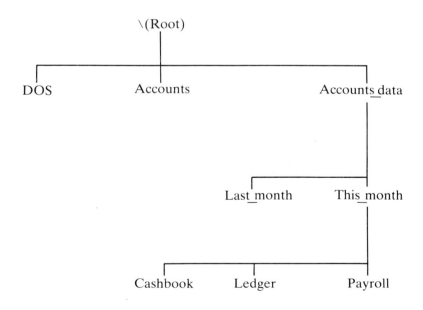

Fig. 5.3. A sample MS-DOS file structure.

Table 5.4. MS-DOS file extensions

.ASM	8086 Assembly language source code
.BAK	Backup file created by EDLIN or some other text editor
.BAS	BASIC source code
.BAT	Batch command file
.COB	Cobol source code
.COM	Executable command file
.DAT	Data file (assumed to be ASCII)
.EXE	Relocatable executable file
.FOR	Fortran source code
.LIB	Library file
.LST	Listing of compilation or assembly
.MAP	List file from linker
.OBJ	Relocatable object module
.PAS	Pascal source file
.PRN	Listing of compilation or assembly
.CRF	Cross reference
.$$$	Temporary system generated file

Directories are identified by their name without a filename aded. Thus

a:\

is the main directory of the disk drive a: and

a:\DOS

is the directory 'DOS' on the disk in drive a:
All disks must be formatted before they are used, and the formatting process includes initializing the root directory (\) on the disk. Subdirectories must be created and managed by the user.
Three commands are involved:
1 MKDIR creates a subdirectory;
2 RMDIR removes a subdirectory;
3 CD or CHDIR changes the default directory (the directory from which files are taken if no other is stated as part of the filename).
Each command takes a directory name as a parameter. So:

MKDIR \DOS

creates the subdirectory '\DOS', and:

RMDIR \DOS

removes it again. Since the removal of a subdirectory would make it impossible to access any files that are held in it, 'RMDIR' will only remove the subdirectory if no files are present.

'CHDIR' changes the default directory. All future commands will use files in the specified subdirectory if no directory is specified. For example:

CHDIR   a:\DOS

changes the default directory on the a: disk to DOS. MS-DOS remembers the current directory for each drive in the system and any reference to that drive will access that directory unless told otherwise.

CHDIR \

makes the root directory of the current drive the default directory. 'CHDIR' without any parameters displays the default directory of the current drive and:

CHDIR <drive>

for example:

CHDIR a:

displays the default directory of the drive specified.

'CD' can be used instead of 'CHDIR'.

5.3.2 Starting Up under MS-DOS

MS-DOS is similar to CP/M in that there is a standard core, which is the same for all microcomputers, and a BIOS which handles the input/output and other features that are different for each microcomputer. These two parts are merged by the microcomputer manufacturer and are then stored in the file 'COMMAND.COM' which must be copied onto the boot diskette. Often, a large proportion of the BIOS is placed in 'read-only' memory so that it is always available and does not clutter the microcomputer's main memory.

In addition to the options specified by the microcomputer manufacturer, MS-DOS has several installation-specific settings to be configured at a system startup.

The MS-DOS configuration file 'CONFIG.SYS' allows you to configure your system with a minimum of effort. With this file you can add device drivers to your system at startup. The configuration file is simply an ASCII file that has certain commands for MS-DOS startup (boot). The boot process is as follows.

1   The disk boot sector is read. This contains enough code to read MS-DOS code and the installation's BIOS (machine-dependent code).

2   The MS-DOS code and BIOS are read.

3   A system initialization routine reads the configuration file 'CON-FIG.SYS', if it exists, to perform device installation and other user options.

4   Its final task is to execute the command interpreter, which executes the commands listed in the file 'AUTOEXEC.BAT' before displaying the system prompt, ready to accept commands from the user. This finishes the MS-DOS boot process.

The following commands are likely to be found in the 'CONFIG-.SYS' file.

BUFFERS=<number>

This is the number of sector buffers that will comprise the system list. It is installation-dependent and most manufacturers give recommendations about suitable values for their systems, which should generally be followed.

DEVICE=<filename>

This installs the device driver in <filename> into the system list.

SHELL=<filename>

This begins execution of the shell (top-level command processor) from <filename> instead of 'COMMAND.COM'.

COUNTRY=<number>

The country code tells MS-DOS which conventions to use for:
(a)   the date and time format,
(b)   the currency symbol, and
(c)   the decimal separator.
The codes recognized include:

France	033
Germany	049
Italy	039
Spain	034

United Kingdom   044
United States   001

It may be necessary to run a keyboard configuration program from within the 'AUTOEXEC.BAT' file to take account of different keyboard layouts.

A typical configuration file might be:

BUFFERS=16
COUNTRY=044

'CONFIG.SYS' can be modified, if necessary, by the MS-DOS editor EDLIN.

MS-DOS records the date and time that a file was last modified. It is therefore necessary to inform the microcomputer of the current date and time. There are various ways of doing this, depending on which microcomputer is used, the most common being:

(a)   to request the user to type them in as part of the boot process,

(b)   to call the commands 'DATE' and 'TIME' in the 'AUTOEX-EC.BAT' file,

(c)   to obtain the date and time from a built-in battery clock and only use the system commands 'DATE' and 'TIME' when this clock needs to be reset. If no 'AUTOEXEC.BAT' file is present the system prompts the user directly for the current date and time.

In some versions of MS-DOS, 'DATE' and 'TIME' have been combined and are called 'WTDATIM'.

5.3.3 Using MS-DOS

MS-DOS treats disks in the same way as CP/M and labels each with a unique single letter identifier, such as:

a:

It is possible to change the default drive by simply typing the new drive letter followed by a colon (:) in response to the system prompt:

A>

The drive letter will then change and all files without a specific drive prefix will henceforth be read from the new default drive.

Internal Commands

Unlike CP/M, where only the minimum code necessary is loaded into memory when the system is stored, MS-DOS takes advantage of the additional memory space available to load in some of the simpler standard commands. They are known as 'internal commands'. These are then available to the user without the delay associated with loading them from disk, nor is it necessary to ensure that they are available on the current system disk.

MS-DOS internal commands include:

Command name	Command function
COPY	Copies specified file or files
DATE	Sets and displays the date
DEL	Deletes specified file or files
DIR	Lists specified directory entries
PAUSE	Pauses for input in a batch file
REM	Displays a comment in a batch file
REN	Renames a file
TIME	Sets and displays the time
TYPE	Displays the contents of a specified file

and the directory management commands 'MKDIR', 'RMDIR' and 'CHDIR' discussed in Section 5.3.1.

'TIME' and 'DATE' are used to display the current time or date and allow the user to change it.

TYPE <file specification>

displays the contents of a file on the display. So:

TYPE DOCUMENT.TXT

displays the contents of the file 'DOCUMENT.TXT'.

Files are deleted with the 'DEL' command which has the general form:

DEL <file specification>

The <file specification> can be a single filename or a collection of files whose names fit the specified name template. This is done by using the wild card characters '*' and '?' which have the same meaning as in CP/M. For example

DEL PROGRAM.*

will delete all files with the name 'PROGRAM' whatever their extension, and:

DEL CHAPTER?.TXT

deletes files with names such as:

CHAPTER.TXT
CHAPTER1.TXT and
CHAPTERA.TXT

It is possible to delete all the files in the current directory with the command:

DEL *.*

but because of the potentially catastrophic consequences, MS-DOS asks for confirmation before removing all the files.

As with CP/M, it is not possible to delete the files on more than one disk at the same time.

The files held in a particular directory can be displayed with the 'DIR' command which has the form:

DIR <directory>

in which case all the files in the directory are displayed, or:

DIR <file specification>

when only those files that meet the file specification are displayed.

For example:

DIR

displays all the files in the current default directory,

DIR c:

displays all the files in the default directory or drive c:, and:

DIR CHAPTER*.TXT

displays all the files with the extension 'TXT' and names starting with 'CHAPTER' in the current default directory.

Files can be renamed with the 'REN' (or 'RENAME') command which has the form:

REN <old filename> <new filename>

A drive and directory can be specified only for the <old filename> since after renaming the file will remain in the same directory.

Examples are:

REN CHAPTER.BAK OLDCHAP.TXT

will rename 'CHAPTER.BAK' as 'OLDCHAP.TXT', and:

REN CHAPTER.BAK *.TXT

will rename it 'CHAPTER.TXT'

MS-DOS provides a powerful 'COPY' command which can be used to copy single files or groups of files. Its general form is:

COPY <source file specification> <destination file specification>

For example:

COPY CHAPTER.TXT OLDCHAP.TXT

copies the contents of 'CHAPTER.TXT' into the file 'OLD-CHAP.TXT'. If no destination filename is given then the original filename is used. This is a convenient method of copying selected files to new directories or another disk. For example:

COPY CHAPTER?.TXT\BACKUP

copies files with names such as:

CHAPTER.TXT
CHAPTER1.TXT and
CHAPTERA.TXT

into the directory '\BACKUP' in the current default disk, and:

COPY CHAPTER?.TXT B:

will copy these files from the current default drive to the disk in the B: drive. A useful facility offered by the 'COPY' command is to enter text directly into a file. This is done by using 'CON' (the console keyboard) as the source filename. For example:

COPY CON   AUTOEXEC.BAT

can be used to create an 'AUTOEXEC.BAT' file. The text to be placed in the file is then typed, finishing with an end-of-file character (CTRL -Z).

External Commands

Only the most common or simplest commands can be included in MS-DOS as internal commands. Special commands that are used less frequently are stored on diskette and loaded only when required. They are known as 'External Commands'.

The program files contain the extension .COM or .EXE but are called by just their name without any extension.

Examples of MS-DOS external commands include:

FORMAT   prepares new disks for use and, optionally, creates a new system disk.

CHKDSK   scans the directory of a disk and checks it for consistency.

COMP   compares the contents of files.

DISKCOPY   copies the total contents of a disk.

EDLIN   the MS-DOS line-oriented text file editor.

TREE   displays the directory structure of a disk.

The command name can be preceded by a drive letter if the command is not on the disk in the current default drive, and subdirectory names, as necessary.

It is often useful to hide the command files in subdirectories independent of the main system defaults. This allows command files to be separated from data and applications files in the main disk directory and user-created subdirectories. This is accomplished by use of the 'PATH' command. This takes one parameter which is a list of the directories that are to be searched for commands that were not found in the current default directory, separated by (;). So, for example, if all the MS-DOS external commands are held in a subdirectory called '\DOS' on the system diskette in drive A: and also its main directory, a suitable command to add to the 'AUTOEXEC.BAT' file would be:

PATH = a:\;a:\DOS

the search path can be reset to null (that is, no further directories will be searched after the current working directory) by:

PATH ;

and the current 'path' can be displayed by typing:

PATH

Batch Files

It is often necessary to type the same sequence of commands.

With MS-DOS, the command sequence can be placed in a special file and the entire sequence executed by simply typing the name of the batch file. The commands in such files are obeyed as if they were typed at the terminal.

Each batch file is given a '.BAT' extension. It is executed by typing the filename only, without its extension. You can create a batch file by using the line editor (EDLIN), or by using the COPY command.

Input and Output Redirection

Most commands produce output that is sent to the microcomputer's screen. To send this information to a file, a greater than sign (>) can be used. For example, the command

DIR

lists a directory onto the microcomputer. The same command can be used to send this information to a file. For example:

DIR > THESE_FILES

If the file 'THESE_FILES' does not already exist, MS-DOS creates it and stores the directory listing in it. If 'THESE_FILES' already exists, MS-DOS overwrites what is in the file with the new information.

If the information is to be added at the end of an existing file, two greater than signs (>>) are used. For example, the command:

DIR >> THESE_FILES

appends your directory listing to a currently existing file named 'THESE_FILES'. If 'THESE_FILES' does not exist, it is created.

It is often useful to have input for a program come from a file rather than from the keyboard. This is possible in MS-DOS by using a less than sign (<) in your command. For example, the command

SORT <NAMES > NAMES_LIST

sorts the file 'NAMES' and sends the sorted output to a file named 'NAMES_LIST'.

Filters

A filter is a command that reads input, transforms it in some way, and then outputs it to the terminal screen or to a file. Since filters can be put together in different ways, a few filters can take the place of many specific commands.

MS-DOS filters include 'FIND', 'MORE', and 'SORT'. Their functions are:

(a)   FIND   Searches for a string of text in a file.
(b)   MORE   Takes standard output and displays it, one screen at a time.
(c)   SORT   Sorts text alphabetically.

If more than one command is required, then output can be 'piped' from one to the next. Piping is done by separating commands with the pipe separator, which is the vertical bar symbol (|). For example, the command:

DIR | SORT

will give an alphabetically sorted listing of the current directory. The vertical bar causes all output generated by the left side of the bar to be sent to the right side of the bar for processing.

A pipeline may consist of more than two programs. For example:

DIR | SORT | MORE

will sort the current directory, show it to you one screen at a time, and put --MORE-- at the bottom of the screen when there is more output to be seen.

When 'pipes' are used the microcomputer uses the disk in the default drive to hold temporary files (with an extension of '.$$$'). This disk must therefore have sufficient free space available, and must not be write-protected, otherwise an unexpected 'DISK FULL' error message will be displayed.

5.4 Unix

Unix is different from CP/M and MS-DOS in that it is designed to support multiple users initiating more than one concurrent task. Even in single-user systems the multi-tasking facilities provided allow the user to perform both foreground and background tasks. It is, therefore, possible to edit one file while paginating and printing another. This is different from spooling printout since it includes active pagination.

Unix originated during the previous computer revolution. In the late 1960s minicomputers were becoming fairly widespread, but there was little software available for them. Between 1965 and 1969 Bell Laboratories had been involved with General Electric (now Honeywell) and Project MAC at the Massachusetts Institute of Technology in the development of the Multics operating system. This was a large and complex system intended to serve the diverse needs of large user communities. Such a system requires a large computer (originally a GE-645 mainframe).

When Bell Laboratories withdrew from the Multics project in 1969 some members of the team started work on a much less ambitious project to run on a spare DEC PDP-7 minicomputer. This team was led by Ken Thompson and it was written in assembler. The first version of Unix was thus born.

Two basic design features that were later to predominate in the design of Unix were already apparent. These were that:
1 from the start Unix was developed within the Unix environment. This made the Unix team the first and, for a long time, the largest Unix users. They therefore had an immediate need to provide a complete system. The maintenance of an integrated system was also to aid portability later;
2 the Unix team was always to consist of a small number of experts. The designers were also major users of the system. This meant that deficiencies were rapidly detected (often by the designer himself) and soon corrected. This was different from other operating systems which were designed by systems analysts and coded by armies of comparatively unskilled programmers with the result that the user got what the manufacturer thought he should have, rather than what he really wanted.

At this stage Dennis Ritchie became involved. It was decided to port Unix to the more modern DEC PDP-11 series of minicomputers. As much of the software as possible was rewritten in a high-level language called C. This greatly aided portability.

PDP-11s were already very popular in the universities. News of Unix was spreading fast, and in 1973 Western Electric (Bell Laboratories' parent) agreed to licence it to non-profit making organizations. Unix was soon in use in universities around the world. This was the start of Unix's popularity.

The first Unix to become generally available was Version 5. This looked more like the output of a research project than a production operating system. Version 6 appeared in 1975 and Version 7 was released in 1979. The C source for the operating system and all its utilities was released with the system so that bugs were soon corrected locally and enhancements filtered back to Bell Laboratories from sites all over the world.

Unix was soon ported to other processors. The high proportion of C code greatly assisted this since once a suitable C compiler was available only a comparatively small amount of low-level code needed to be rewritten in assembler. Notable ports have been to DEC VAX computers by both Bell Laboratories, the University of California (Berkeley) and to the Motorola 68000 microprocessor by Bell Laboratories. More details of some of the common Unix versions available are given in Section 5.4.3.

Since Version 7 was released Bell Laboratories have changed their policy on distribution and maintenance. With the announcement of System III in 1981 Bell introduced a new pricing policy which included binary sub-licences for as little as $100. As well as consolidating the best in the previous (incompatible) versions, accounting facilities were introduced for the first time, which is an essential feature for commercial users.

In January 1983 the current Bell issue, System V, was formally announced. For the first time users outside Bell Laboratories were using the same system as those inside Bell Laboratories. Apart from adding extra libraries and facilities, Bell also started to add some of the Berkeley Unix extensions, notably the 'vi' screen editor, and made considerable improvements to the 'uucp' Unix-to-Unix file communication package.

Current plans are to develop System V to include all the useful features of the other Unix versions (notable Berkeley 4.2) and to make this the 'standard Unix'. To this end, System V Release 2 became available in 1984 with:

(a) improved job control,

(b) improved shell performance, and

(c) new networking packages.

In addition, it is likely that the current method of distributing Unix will change, in that instead of having to take all or nothing, a range of licences will be introduced giving access to a range of different facilities. This will make it much more convenient to build commercial software around the Unix core.

5.4.1 The Structure of Unix

Unix consists of a small kernel surrounded by a series of utilities. When a Unix-based system is ported to run on another system the major part of the work is to adapt the kernel to the new hardware requirements. The newly developed kernel will then accept standard Unix interfaces and system calls, and perform the required actions on the new hardware. It is the responsibility of the kernel in the operating system to decide how to access devices such as printers and disk files. It therefore performs a similar function as the BIOS in CP/M and MS-DOS.

The Unix Command Environment

There are nearly two hundred commands available as part of the standard Unix operating system. These commands:

(a)   create and maintain files and directories,

(b)   create file systems,

(c)   mount and demount file systems,

(d)   link files across directories,

(e)   communicate with other users,

(f)   edit, compile and debug programs,

(g)   process files in various ways, and

(h)   perform text processing operations.

It is a basic feature of the Unix philosophy that each command performs just one task. The power of the system is that each of these commands can be linked into an appropriate sequence to perform more complex tasks. When appropriate standard tools are not available only those functions that cannot be performed by them need be written as programs. They are then used in conjunction with the appropriate standard tools to perform the other operations. This avoids the necessity of duplicating large sections of code in different programs, with consequent improvements in both the speed of development and the maintainability of the complete system.

Bourne Shell

The Bourne shell is one of the most common user interfaces to Unix. A shell is a command language interpreter and acts as the interface between any user and the rest of the system. It interprets commands, calls the corresponding programs into memory, and then executes them. The shell is itself a full programming language and can be used to create new commands simply by writing shell scripts (often called shell procedures). These shell scripts can be used in exactly the same way as any other program or command. The shell language contains flow-control constructs such as:

'if...then...else...fi'
'case...in...esac'
'for...do...done'
'while...do...done'
'until...do...done'

It also allows the definition of variables, the passing of parameters, and the processing of software signals (or software interrupts).

Both programs and shell scripts are called by the shell in the same way. This allows them to be used interchangeably by the user, giving a highly consistent user interface. Since it is in practice very much easier to write and debug shell scripts, experienced Unix programmers often use them instead of writing programs.

Input/Output Redirection and Pipelines

The Unix shell structure provides a uniform means for redirecting input and output of individual commands. The standard input is the keyboard and the standard output is the display. Either, or both, of these can be replaced by using the redirection facilities similar to those available within MS-DOS. Input can be collected from a file rather than the terminal keyboard. So, whereas:

    sort

will sort a series of lines typed in at the keyboard into alphabetical order, and display the output on the screen,

    sort <index

takes the input from the file 'index' and displays the output on the screen. Similarly, output redirection is performed using the '>' operator. For example, the command:

    echo "Hello there"

will display the message

    Hello there

on the terminal display. This message can be placed in the file 'my-messages' by using the command:

    echo "Hello there" > my-messages

In this example the contents of 'my-messages' is replaced by the new message. It is often necessary to add the new text to the end of the current file contents. This is done by using the '>>' operator:

    echo "Hello there" >> my-messages

This is particularly useful in maintaining log files to give information about the usage of different commands.

Some Unix commands generate error messages when things go wrong. These are usually directed to the terminal display. Even when output indirection is in force these messages are not affected. This is because error messages are only produced when things are disastrously wrong and the user will usually need to know about them. It is possible, however, to redirect this output to a file using the '2>' operator. So:

    sort <index 2> errors

will sort the contents of the file 'index' and display the result on the screen, but any errors will be reported in the file 'errors'. By using this feature, the input to a command can come from the keyboard, another peripheral device, from a file stored on a disk, or from another program, and still look like the standard input. Similarly, the output from a command can be redirected from the display to the printer, a disk file, or another command.

Another powerful Unix feature which is also available in the MS-DOS is the ability to pipe data from one command to another. Two or more connected programs are known as a pipeline. The shell can thus execute a sequence of commands, with the output of each command becoming the input to the next one in the sequence. This ability to pipe commands not only almost eliminates the need to create temporary workfiles, but minimizes the need to develop special programs for new applications. For example, an application involving sorting of an index file consisting of a series of words, stored one per line, and printing the results, can use two existing Unix programs piped together as follows:

sort index | lpr

The vertical bar is the pipe symbol. The meaning of this pipeline is:
(a)   sort the file named 'index', and then
(b)   print the output of sort on the printer using the lpr command.

Unix Files

The Unix filing system, unlike many others, does not impose any assumptions of how a particular file is structured on the user. All internal structure is imposed by the programs that use that file, not by the filing system itself. This leads to a comparatively simple and very elegant user interface to the filing system. It does, however, lead to some unexpected dangers. It is possible, for instance, to attempt to modify a machine code load module with a text editor. This can cause some most unfortunate results! It is the user's responsibility to ensure that the files used are appropriate for the task in hand. It must be admitted that this is a problem with most filing systems, only with Unix the system does not enforce any system of file suffixes in the same way as CP/M or MS-DOS. What it does mean is that you are not, for instance, tied to one text editor. If it is more appropriate for a particular task to use another tool, this can be accomplished without difficult file conversion operations.

Some Unix utilities define standard file suffixes so that special types of files can be readily identified. These include:
(a)   .c   source programs written in C

(b) .f   source programs written in Fortran
(c) .o   compiled programs before they are turned into executable
               form.

In addition, other software suppliers use similar suffixes to identify their own file types. Common examples are:

(a) .p   } Pascal source files
     .pas

(b) .dat   data file
(c) .idx   index file (databases, etc.).

The Unix file system consists of files and directories; it allows file-names up to at least fourteen alphanumeric characters in length and differentiates between uppercase and lowercase.

Directories help group files for easy reference or separation. The Unix file system, which is a hierarchical file system, consists of many levels of hierarchies, i.e. directories within directories. Figure 5.4 is an example of such a hierarchical file system.

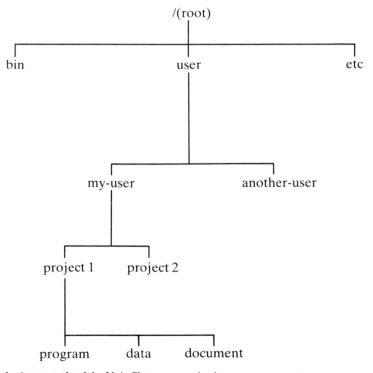

Fig. 5.4. An example of the Unix filestore organization.

The Unix file system has a unique path for each file in the system. This unique path — also called the absolute filename — is the name of the file in relation to the root of the file system. The root of the file system is the slash symbol (/). Within the Unix file system some directories are standard and contain Unix command files. Some of these are:

(a) /(the root directory) Must be present in all Unix file structures and is the ancestor of all files in the filing system.

(b) /usr   Each user's home directory is typically a sub-directory of /usr.

(c) /bin and /usr/bin   Contain the standard Unix utility programs. By convention, /bin contains all the frequently used utilities including those needed to bring the system up, whereas the more obscure utilities are stored in /usr/bin.

(d) /dev   Contains files that represent the physical devices such as terminals and printers connected to the system.

(e) /etc   Contains administrative and configuration programs, together with other system files.

(f) /tmp   Contains temporary files generated by many Unix programs.

Unlike CP/M and MS-DOS, Unix keeps track of the disk on which files reside. The user does not need to specify a drive letter as part of the filename.

Each user of the Unix system must be assigned his own directory in which to store his own files. This is created by adding an entry in the file:

    /etc/password

which stores information that the system requires when a user logs on. This includes:

(a) the user name,

(b) the home directory that is used when the user first logs in, and

(c) the user's password in encrypted form.

This file can be read by any user, which at first sight appears to be a major security breach. However, the encryption algorithm used is so efficient that it is almost impossible to break. The password is therefore held securely. The user can change his password himself, using the utility:

    password

This password prompts the user for the new password, which is not displayed on the screen. The old password is then requested as an identity check. This is to stop unauthorized users finding a terminal already logged in and changing the password. The user is then asked to repeat the new password, to ensure that it had not been mistyped, and if all is well it is encrypted and '/etc/password' is updated. Otherwise an error message informs the user that the password has not been changed.

If a user forgets his password the super-user can change his password for him without knowing the old password. The super-user cannot, however, read the old password.

Each file has a set of access permissions associated with it. These consist of three types of user, each with three different means of access, making nine in all. The three types of user are:

(a)   the owner himself,

(b)   other users in the owner's own group, and

(c)   all other users.

A group is a collection of users defined by the super-user. It is most likely to be a small group of users working on the same project who need to share some information between themselves.

Since Unix is a multi-user system where any user can gain access to the computer from all terminals, the new user must introduce himself to Unix by responding to the login prompt:

Login:

with his username. Unix then responds with the message:

Password:

to which the user responds with his password. This is not displayed on the screen to minimize the chances of unauthorized persons reading it illicitly. If all is well and the username and password match with those recorded in the passwords file, Unix gives the user access to the system.

Before giving the user access to the system, the commands in two special files called

/etc/profile

and,

.profile

in the user's home directory are executed as if they had been typed in directly before control is passed to the terminal.

The first is set up by the system administrator and is used to provide a general environment for all users. This may include:

(a)   displaying a message to confirm that the user has successfully logged on and to say which machine he is using;

(b)   setting up defaults for various shell parameters;

(c)   displaying a 'news' file giving information of general interest to users;

(d)   after 'etc/profile' has been executed Unix then tries to find the file:
      .profile

in the user's own login directory. This allows each user to provide a series of commands which tailor the standard environment to meet his needs.

The '.' at the start of the filename means that it will not appear in standard Unix directory listings.

The most common uses are:

(a)   to set up a special 'PATH' or directory search path for Unix commands;

(b)   to change various system settings to make the best use of special terminals. (The system administrator sets the system up so that it can be used from the simplest terminal available, particularly when access is via some sort of computer network. Each user is, however, unlikely to use more than one or two terminals. He is therefore able to set a more sensible default for his own purposes.);

(c)   finding out who else is logged into the system changing the default working directory;

(d)   checking whether any 'mail' has been received.

When the user has finished everything that he wants to do for that particular session it is necessary to log off and return the terminal to the state in which it will allow another user to log into the system. With most versions of Unix this is done by pressing <CTRL-D> in response to the shell prompt.

5.4.2 Some Unix Commands

With nearly two hundred commands in the basic Unix vocabulary, and the almost infinite number of local variants, it is impossible to give more than a general overview of those most commonly met in the space available here. The ease with which Unix command files can be modified, as well as the variations in the different versions of Unix, means that there are invariably considerable differences in the user interface between different computers running Unix. It is usual practice, however, for at least the basic set of commands to be available on any machine.

Even with this apparently very large number of commands, many of them require the user to select various options to make use of all their functions. Unix commands have the general form:

<command name> <options> <parameters>

where the options (if present) are single characters preceded by a minus (−). If more than one option is selected thay can in most cases either be listed separately, with each preceded by a minus (−), or can be put together in one option list, in which case only one minus is required at the beginning of the list.

Listing, Copying and Deleting Files

The listing facility in Unix is the concatenate (cat) command. This has the form:

cat <file list>

where <file list> is a list of files to be output one after another to the output, which is, by default, the terminal. So:

cat book.chapter1

will display the contents of the file 'book.chapter1' on the terminal, and

cat book.chapter1 book.chapter2

will display 'book.chapter2' immediately after 'book.chapter1'. This can be redirected into the file 'book' with the command:

cat book.chapter1 book.chapter2 >book

It is possible to use the 'cat' command to enter text directly into a file, since, if no files are listed as parameters, the input is taken from terminal. The input must be terminated with an end-of-file character (usually <CTRL-Z> or <CTRL-D> but it can be redefined on your system).

So, for example:

cat >test.file
this is a simple message
to test file input
<CTRL-D>

will put the message

this is a simple message
to test file input

into the file 'test.file'.

Output to the system printer is activated by the 'lpr' command. This has the form:

lpr <options> <file list>

Common options are:

(a) −c Copy the file immediately before placing it in the printer queue, so that it cannot be changed.
(b) −r Delete the file immediately after printing.
(c) −m Use the 'mail' utility to inform the user when the file is finished printing.

'lpr' can be used as a filter, in which case it takes no file parameter, so that:

cat book.chapter1 book.chapter2 lpr

will print the contents of 'book.chapter1' followed by the contents of 'book.chapter2', or the filenames can be provided as a parameter list:

lpr −m book.chapter1 book.chapter2

in which case a mail message will be sent to inform the user when the files have been printed.

'lpr' does not divide the output into pages or do any other processing that would normally be expected of a file listing function. This is all handled by another utility called 'pr'. This also adds page headers and has the general form:

pr <options> <file list>

Some commonly used options are:

(a)   −h<header>   use <header> instead of the filename in the page header line.

(b)   −n<number>   pages are <number> lines long.

(c)   −m   print all files simultaneously, one file in each column.

(d)   +<number>   begin output at page <number> (the default is start at page 1).

(e)   −w<number> use a page width of <number> characters (the default is 72) for multicolumn output.

Typical uses would be:

        pr book.chapter1 |lpr

would paginate 'book.chapter1' before printing it, or if output was intended to go to a file called 'chapter1.pr':

        pr book.chapter1 >chapter1.pr

If pages only sixty lines long were required, and page numbering starting at page ten were required, then:

        pr −n60+10 book.chapter1

would suffice.

It is possible to copy the contents of a file to another with the 'cp' command:

        cp <source file> <destination file>

so, for example:

        cp a.out bin/new_command

will copy the contents of 'a.out' to 'bin/new_command'.

The move command (mv) operates in a similar way, except that the file is renamed and hence the original is lost:

        mv a.out bin/new_command

It is sometimes useful to be able to refer to a file by two different names. Unix provides a means of doing this with the link command (ln). It is used in the same way as 'mv' and 'cp', but although two entries appear in the relevant directories only one copy of the contents of the file is kept. If the file is modified in any way the same changes will have apparently been made simultaneously to all files linked to it:

ln file1 file2

Once files are no longer required, they should be deleted. This is done with the 'rm' command which has the form:

rm <options> <filename>

With the interactive (−i) option rm requests confirmation from the user before deleting a file.

It is not usually permissible to use rm to remove directories, but when the recursive (−r) option is used and the file parameter is a directory:

rm −r <directory>

the directory and all subdirectories, together with all the files they contain, are deleted. This is an option that must be used with extreme caution.

In addition to the ability to specify individual filenames, the Unix shell allows you to define groups of files by using 'wild card' characters in the same way as CP/M and MS-DOS. These characters are detected by the shell before the parameter is passed to the process and the appropriate filenames are substituted. The wild cards accepted by the Unix shell are:

(a) *   matches any string of characters, including the null string.
(b) ?   matches any single character.
(c) [...]   matches any of the enclosed range of characters '...' in turn. (If two characters appearing in the pattern in alphabetical order are separated by a dash ('−') then any character in the alphabetic range between these two characters will be matched.) In many ways this is a more selective version of the '?' form.

So if it was desired to print out all the files with '.c' and '.h' suffixes, with the appropriate page headers, this could be done with the command:

pr *.[ch] |lpr

If you wanted to delete all the files with the suffix '.o' and a filename of 'pass' followed by a number, this could be done with:

rm pass [0–9].o

This is more specific than using:

rm pass?.o

which would delete not only files with names such as:

pass1.o

and

pass4.o

but also ones with names such as:

passa.o

and

pass..o

as well, which may not be intended.

Listing, Creating and Removing Directories

The Unix directory structure is very powerful because of the ease with which it can be used. Unlike MS-DOS, which maintains a 'root' directory for each disk, Unix maintains only one 'root' directory (/) which is common to all users. It is therefore much easier to move around the system, since it is no longer necessary to known on which disk a file resides. It is possible for a user to change his working directory to any that he has access to, not just directories that he himself owns. This is done with the change directory (cd) commands. This has the general form:

cd <directory name>

If the <directory name> is omitted, the user is returned to his home directory (that is the one that he is in immediately after logging on).

Examples of the use of 'cd' are:

cd

return to the home directory,

> cd /usr/bin/

change the current directory to the system directory '/usr/bin'.

> cd . .

move to the directory level above the current one.

It is always possible to find the full path name of the current working directory by typing:

> pwd

A listing of the files held in a directory is obtained with the 'ls' command which has the form:

> ls <options> <directory>

If no directory is specified, the current directory is used.
Common options are:

(a) −l long list — include information about file access permissions, owner, size and date created (by default, only a list of names is produced).

(b) −t produce the list in chronological order (rather than alphabetical order as is the default).

(c) −a list all files in the directory, including those whose names start with a point (.).

Examples of its use are:

ls −l/usr/bin
produce a long listing of the files in '/usr/bin', and
ls −t chapter [0–9]
lists all of the files in the current directory with names of the form 'chapter<n>' in the order that they were last modified

Directories can be created with the 'mkdir' command, which has the form:

> mkdir <directory list>

Any number of directories can be created with one call to 'mkdir'.
'mkdir' creates two files immediately in the new directory:

(a) .   a special file containing the current file directory, and

(b) ..   contains the directory above the current one.

Neither of these files can be deleted by the user.

'rmdir' is used to remove a directory once its usefulness is over. Before this can be done all user files within it must be deleted. If not, Unix returns an error message and leaves the directory intact. The command has the form:

    rmdir <directory-list>

TEXT EDITORS

Computers are often used to store and manipulate files of text, be they program sources, documents for word- or text-processing, or data.

The versions of Unix therefore come with various text editors as part of the operating system package. Some of those more commonly found are:

(a) ed   is the line editor that is distributed with most version of Unix. As with all Unix tools, 'ed' tells the user the minimum necessary (it does not give prompts, for instance);

(b) ex   is an improved text editor which is claimed to be more user-friendly than 'ed' (that is, it actually tells you what is happening);

(c) sed is a special editor for including in shell scripts. Commands are given to it in a similar manner to 'ed';

(d) vi   is a screen editor which is distributed with Berkeley 4.1, Berkeley 4.2 and System V. It works successfully with most common terminals with cursor addressing capability, as well as providing its own screen editing environment.

'ed' and 'sed' will be found in almost all versions of Unix currently distributed; the others will depend on where your version came from. Various manufacturers provide their own text editors for compatibility with their other machine ranges, and it is possible to purchase, or otherwise acquire, a whole range of other text editors including some very sophisticated pieces of software.

5.4.3 Versions of Unix

The popularity of Unix has spawned a whole host of variants of it for a wide range of different computer systems. This came about because AT & T (Bell Laboratories) could not charge for Unix and so released it without any form of support whatsoever. This led to a number of software houses either taking Bell Laboratories code and rewriting

Table 5.5. Some common Unix variants.

Name	Origin	Processor	How produced
4.1 bsd	University of	VAX, Sun,	Partial rewrite with additions.
4.2 bsd	California, Berkeley	Orion	Some additions have been fed back into System V
CTIX	Convergent Technologies	MC68000	Unix port (System V) hosted on its own operating systems (CTOS)
Eunice	SRI	VAX	Emulation under VMS
Genix	National Semiconductor	16032	Unix port
HP-UX	Hewlett-Packard	Various HP machines	Unix port
Idris	Whitesmiths	PDP 11, MC68000	Total rewrite
IX	Apollo	Domain	Unix port (System V) and Berkeley 4.2 concurrent with own operating system (REGIS)
PNX	ICL	Perq	Unix port (Version 7)
System III	Bell Labs (AT & T)	PDP-11, VAX	Being superseded by System V
System V	Bell Labs (AT & T)	PDSP-11, VAX, MC68000	Current system with full support
TNIX	Tektronix	Tektronix	Unix port
UTS	Amdahl	Amdahl VM470	Unix port
Version 6	Bell Labs (AT & T)	PDP-11	Obsolete — superseded by Version 7
Version 7	Bell Labs (AT & T)	PDP-11	Obsolete — superseded by System III
Xenix	Microsoft	8086, MC68000 (including IBM-PC AT)	Unix port (Version 7) plus enhancements
Zeus	Zilog	Zilog Micros (Z80, Z80000)	Unix port plus enhancements

sections of it to produce a much more reliable and maintainable product, or by writing their own operating system with the Unix user
interface. Both of these actions have led to a diversity of different
Unix's all to some extent incompatible. To these must be added the
official ports of Bell Laboratories software. This has led to some considerable confusion in the market place as to what is the 'real' Unix.

This confusion will only be resolved with the establishment of appropriate standards. At the time of writing there are groups working on international standards for:

(a) the C programming language,

(b) C library routines, and

(c) the interface between user programs and the Unix kernel.

If acceptable standards are established much of the current confusion should be resolved very quickly since most of the software problems are due to low-level incompatibilities in these areas.

Most of the major computer manufacturers have announced some form of Unix implementation. Where manufacturers have been reluctant to do so, third-party suppliers have often stepped in. Table 5.5 gives some of the more widely available variants, together with the processors on which they run.

5.5 Bibliography

Deitel H.M. (1984) *An Introduction to Operating Systems*. Addison-Wesley.
Lister A.M. (1984) *Fundamentals of Operating Systems*, 3rd edn. Macmillan.
Peterson J. & Silberschatz A. (1983) *Operating Systems Concepts*. Addison-Wesley.

5.5.1 CP/M

Blackburn L. & Taylor M. (1984) *Pocket Guide to CP/M*. Pitman.
Clarke A., Eaton J.M. & Powys-Lybbe D. (1983) *CP/M The Software Bus*. Sigma Technical Press.
Dahmke M. (1983) *The BYTE Guide to CP/M-86*. Byte Books/McGraw-Hill.
Dwyer T. & Critchfield M. (1983) *CP/M and the Personal Computer*. Addison-Wesley.
Zaks R. (1980) *The CP/M Handbook with MP/M*. Sybex.

5.5.2 MS-DOS

Eager B. (1984) *Introduction to PC-DOS*. Addison-Wesley.
Hoffman P. & Nicoloff T. (1985) *The Osborne/McGraw-Hill MS-DOS User's Guide*. McGraw-Hill.
King V. & Waller D. (1984) *Pocket Guide to MS-DOS*. Pitman.
Lucy S. (1984) *The MS-DOS User Book*. Sigma Technical Press.
Sheldon T. (1985) *Introducing PC-DOS*. Byte Books/McGraw-Hill.
Slade A. (1984) *PC-DOS for the Experienced User*. Addison-Wesley.

5.5.3 Unix

Blackburn L. & Taylor M. (1984) *Pocket Guide to Unix*. Pitman.
Bourne S.R. (1982) *The Unix System*. Addison-Wesley.
Brown P. (1984) *Starting with Unix*. Addison-Wesley.
Budgen D. (1985) *Making Use of Unix*. Edward Arnold.
Miller C. & Boyle R. (1984) *Unix for Users*. Blackwell Scientific Publications.
Sorbell M.G. (1984) *A Practical Guide to Unix*. Benjamin/Cummings.
Sorbell M.G. (1985) *A Practical Guide to Unix System V*. Benjamin/Cummings.
Thomas R. & Yates J. (1982) *A User Guide to the Unix System*. Osborne/McGraw-Hill.
Yates J. & Emerson S. (1984) *A Business Guide to the Xenix System*. Addison-Wesley.
also *Bell Systems Technical Journal*, vol. 57, No.6, Part 2, July–August 1978. This is a special edition, all about Unix.

Appendix:
Trademarks

This book makes many references to words which are trademarks. These are listed below. If there are any errors or omissions in the list, these will be corrected and included in future editions.

CP/M, CP/M-80, CP/M-86, CCP/M, CP/M-68K, Concurrent and GEM are trademarks of Digital Research Inc.

MS-DOS and MS-WINDOWS are trademarks of Microsoft Corp.

PC-DOS and TOPVIEW are trademarks of IBM Inc.

UNIX is a trademark of Bell Laboratories.

XENIX is a trademark of Microsoft Corp.

Macintosh is a trademark of Apple Computer Inc.

Multics is a trademark of Honeywell Computer Systems.

TELETYPE is a trademark of Teletype Corporation.

Index

Titles in the series

A SNOWY DAY   WHAT CAN I HEAR?
A STORMY DAY   WHAT CAN I SEE?
A SUNNY DAY   WHAT CAN I TASTE?
A WINDY DAY   WHAT CAN I TOUCH?

CLEAN AND DIRTY   COTTON
HOT AND COLD   GLASS
LIGHT AND DARK   RUBBER
WET AND DRY   WOOD

BEANS
BREAD
FRUIT
VEGETABLES

British Library Cataloguing in Publication Data

Petty, Kate
Rubber.
1. Rubber
I. Title   II. Baker, Madeleine   III. Series
678′2

ISBN 0-340-50392-0

First published 1990

Published by Hodder and Stoughton Children's Books,
a division of Hodder and Stoughton Ltd,
Mill Road, Dunton Green, Sevenoaks, Kent TN13 2YA

Printed in Italy

RUBBER

Kate Petty

Illustrated by Madeleine Baker

HODDER AND STOUGHTON
LONDON SYDNEY AUCKLAND TORONTO

Rubber is funny stuff.
It can bend and stretch and
spring back into shape.

Elastic is made from threads
of rubber. Elastic keeps
Sophie's clothes up. It keeps
her hair tidy, too.

Play with a rubber balloon
to find out what else makes
rubber such a useful material.

It is stretchy,

and airtight,

strong,

waterproof,

and bouncy.

Have you found out
anything else?

5

What is rubber?

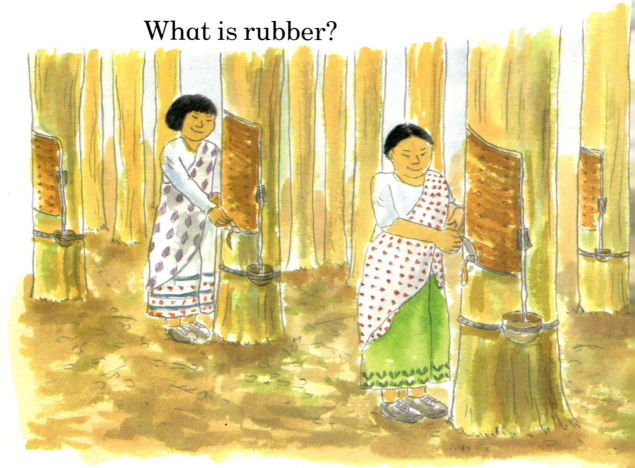

Natural rubber comes from a tree. It is a milky liquid found under the bark. The bark is cut and the liquid is collected in cups.

This Malaysian family
grows its own rubber trees.
Everybody helps with
the work.

Synthetic rubber is made
in a factory. It looks like
natural rubber.

All rubber has to be mixed
with other ingredients,

shaped, and 'cooked'

before it is ready to use.

Sophie watches the tennis players. They wear shoes with rubber soles to stop them slipping. Tennis balls are made with rubber.

Look how the tennis ball
changes shape as it bounces.

Bounce all sorts of balls and
see what happens.

Most rubber is used for making tyres. How many vehicles can you think of that run smoothly on rubber tyres?

Windscreen wipers and many
other car parts are also made
of rubber.

Sophie's boots kept her feet dry
in the rain. Now her dad fills
a hot-water bottle to keep her
feet warm in bed.

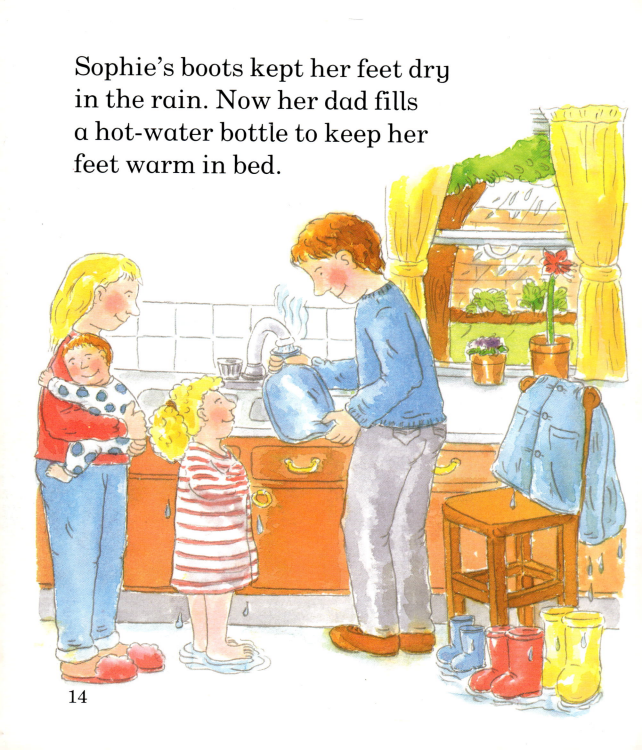

Because rubber is waterproof, it is very useful around the house. Rubber gloves are made by dipping hand-shaped 'formers' into liquid rubber.

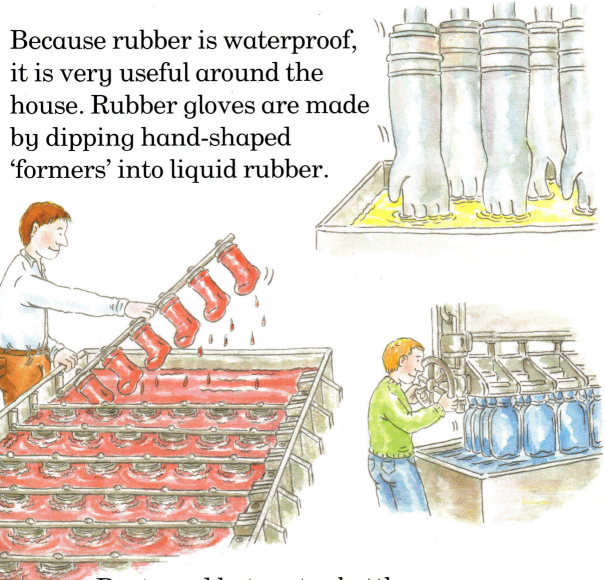

Boots and hot-water bottles are also made this way.

All sorts of small everyday objects are made from rubber. Look at the baby's bottle, Sophie's eraser, and even the sticky bit of sticky tape.

A fridge door is sealed with
a rubber strip to keep the
cold air in. What other doors
might be sealed with rubber?

Sophie watches a TV programme about deep-sea divers. They wear rubber suits to keep out the cold as well as the wet.

Have you got a pair of flippers or
goggles? They are flexible and
fit comfortably because they are
made of rubber.

Bedtime for Sophie. Her soft mattress and pillows are made from foam rubber. Foam rubber is full of air bubbles.

There is a layer of foam rubber
under Sophie's carpet, too. Mum
can tiptoe out very quietly.

There are at least 15 things in this picture made of rubber. Can you spot them all? The answers are on the opposite page.

rubber words

balloon

boots

foam rubber

rubber gloves

rubber tree

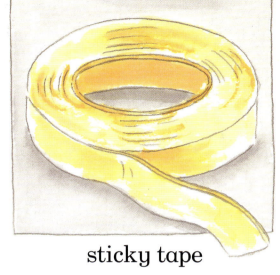

sticky tape

tyre

wetsuit